Body of Truth

Leveraging What Consumers Can't or Won't Say

DAN HILL

WILEY

JOHN WILEY & SONS, INC.

Published by John Wiley & Sons, Inc., Hoboken, New Jersey.
Published simultaneously in Canada.

For general information on our other products and services please contact our Customer
Care Department within the U.S. at (800) 762-2974, outside the United States at (317)
572-3993 or fax (317) 572-4002.

Wiley also publishes its books in a variety of electronic formats. Some content that appears
in print may not be available in electronic books. For more information about Wiley products, visit our Web site at www.Wiley.com.

ISBN: 0-471-44439-1

Printed in the United States of America.

10 9 8 7 6 5 4 3 2 1

CONTENTS

INTRODUCTION

Laying the Groundwork for Sensory Logic

- "Conscious thought is the tip of an enormous iceberg. It is the rule of thumb among cognitive scientists that unconscious thought is 95 percent of all thought—and that may be a serious underestimate."[1]

- Linguists estimate that at least 80 percent of human communication is nonverbal.[2]

- "One rule of thumb used in communications research is that 90 percent or more of an emotional message is nonverbal."[3]

- Two-thirds of all stimuli reaching the brain is visual.[4]

Science has yielded startling insights into how people actually think and communicate. However, these insights haven't yet filtered into the realm of marketing and how consumer behavior is understood.

1

Most marketing efforts still hinge on the idea that consumers are rational beings who can be sold on a product's utilitarian benefits and who can openly articulate their responses to a service or product.

Surprised? Intrigued? Then get comfortable, settle in, and read on. What I have to say is likely to rock the very foundation of how you conduct business on a daily basis if your job involves marketing, advertising, branding, marketing research, public relations, communications, sales, customer service, product design and development, retail design, or other ways that companies and agencies seek to connect more fully with consumers to increase market share.

Armed with this knowledge, you will have an opportunity to be a champion. This book will enable you to make your company or agency more effective in the marketplace, in which the ability to reach, win over, and hold onto consumers spells success.

Getting Back to the Basics

Executives love to talk about getting back to the basics. Well, there is nothing more basic than both the literal physicality of the consumer and the product or service experience itself. So to forge a truly effective marketing relationship with consumers, companies must learn to communicate with consumers on deeper levels—specifically, the physical, the sensory, and the emotional.

This book is titled *Body of Truth* because reading and responding to the human body provides the surest way to connect with consumers. There is much consumers can't or won't say, although they unconsciously have very profound reactions to things. Below the surface of rational thought, the five senses interpret the world, and they dictate emotional responses to the environment and different stimuli.

What's wrong with the old views on consumer behavior, such as the belief in the value of focus groups? These traditional concepts act as if people are creatures only above the neck. Part of the reason marketers have stood by these concepts is because it's far easier to defend rational reasons in a boardroom presentation. In past marketing efforts, many have overestimated the supreme isolated power of reason.

The truth is that people are creatures above *and* below the neck. We're body, heart, and mind—and the body has a logic of its own. Scientific research now indicates that rational thought serves as much to affirm decisions that we've already made emotionally as it does to make decisions on its own. In other words, emotions draw a picture of the world and reason colors it in.

Let me use an illustration from my personal experience with rational marketing efforts. About a decade ago, I was a novice in the business world, about to be led in the wrong direction. I had landed a job in marketing that had among its responsibilities serving as co-chairperson for my company's identity task force. Branding, focus groups, deliverables, limousine rides into New York City to meet with our agency . . . everything was new to me.

With all of the talk about the latest marketing theories, nothing could have prepared us for the results for phase one of our first studies. It turned out there weren't any results. (One woman gave an amusing response when asked what color our company made her think of: beige. I got a laugh, but not many insights.)

Four years later, I was introduced to a revolutionary concept. An acquaintance at IBM faxed over a new article from *American Demographics*.[5] The topic was breakthroughs in brain science and the revolutionary implications for business, including but not limited to marketing research.

As I read the article, I became excited and inspired. This piece changed the course of my career. Now I've launched a company of my own based on what I read. I've honed cutting-edge proprietary tools to gain real consumer insights, and I've created a branding methodology with substance. Most of all, I've continued to study science and psychology to understand more about how companies can connect with consumers most effectively.

I'll support my arguments throughout this book by drawing from advanced research methods, including biofeedback and facial coding, as well as the latest research into how the human brain works. I've used these methods and insights to help such companies as Target, Goodyear, U-Haul, PetSmart, Radisson, Lowe's, 7-Eleven, and Sherwin-Williams. Together, we've come up with new ways to reach customers by appealing to their senses, creating branding efforts centered on an intriguing story, and conducting market research that reveals consumers' true feelings about different products and services. We've had some phenomenal successes, as I'll discuss throughout the book, and we've been able to capitalize fully on some of the latest scientific findings about cognition and communication to reach consumers.

Step Closer, Step Ahead

The slogan of my company and the purpose of this book is as follows: Step closer (to consumers), step ahead (of the competition).

To help you make this happen, first I'll guide you to a better understanding of how people perceive and respond to the commercial world around them. I'll also outline the criteria for how you can close the gap between companies and consumers. This brings me now to the book's subtitle: leveraging what consumers can't or won't say. This is critical, because if you don't know how communication really works, you can't get closer to consumers. You won't be on target, and your messages will be lost on them. Most important, you won't win in the marketplace. It's really as simple as this: The stronger the connection with consumers, the greater the opportunity to create buy-in.

Real, connective communication is crucial. Without it, a company is stuck just talking to itself and wasting a lot of money devising and trying to sell products and services. Getting the message across, however, isn't easy.

Knowing how well the message was received, if it is received at all, is even harder to know for sure. There are responses that consumers *can't* say and those they *won't* say.

Here's my big assertion: People lie. Or at least aren't always candid. Sometimes these are bold, malicious lies. Sometimes these are fairly harmless acts of evasion. It's critical to know the truth from the lies.

The motivation for lying is as varied as human nature. A person can lie because he or she wants to make nice, because he or she is afraid of sounding dumb. Other motivations include lack of involvement or sheer inability to articulate thoughts. People spin, deflect, hint, or hold back all the time and for many reasons, often unintentional.

The problem is even more complex than it first sounds—even if consumers want to cooperate fully, they can't. They don't really know their own minds. Nobody does all the time.

> *Scientists are now able to use neuro-imaging to "eavesdrop"
> on the brain while it's in the act of thinking.*

Their conclusion is that the vast majority of human mental activity is unconscious. It occurs below the surface of our awareness.

Old Challenges, New Opportunities

Nearly everyone in business is affected by how humans withhold information, and how they actually think and communicate. In this book, there are three specific areas I'm going to concentrate on: The first is marketing. I include here anyone whose job influences consumer perceptions of a company. During the 20th century, this field was dominated by a rational, utilitarian orientation. A features, attributes, and benefits approach was the norm—that is, the belief that consumers are rational beings who make decisions based on something like a description of the products' superior performance. Reason-based, neoclassical economics was the underlying dogma bolstering this school of thought.

Identifying additional, differentiating features, attributes, and benefits of the product used to be the challenge. More recently, emotion-based behavioral economics has changed this mandate. Now there is touch-and-feel–oriented "experiential" marketing, which has created the opportunity to use vivid sensory impressions that will lead to the optimal emotional response in consumers.

The second area that's been affected by how consumers actually communicate and make decisions is marketing research. As mentioned, marketers have long regarded focus groups as a reliable way of testing products. I'll show why this is the wrong approach and how we can ascertain how consumers actually make decisions to buy.

My company has pioneered new technologies for understanding how consumers respond on a visceral and sensory-emotive level to different products. As I'll discuss, getting to sensory and emotional reactions—in real time, through the body—is the new big opportunity in marketing research.

Finally, how consumers actually think has profound implications for branding efforts. The earliest phase of branding was all about getting the company's name on the product. The second phase has been largely a matter of getting the company's message on the airwaves and making sure that this exposure didn't go to waste. Now, marketers must learn to apply the new scientific insights by creating a holistic brand story. Every touch point counts, and marketers must learn to bring all the marketing executions together into a story with a vivid mental setting. With compelling characters and a meaningful plot, an effective brand story can draw consumers in, causing them to identify with the brand on emotional terms through situations that they can literally visualize. Engaging consumers on such an emotional level can lead to deep and lasting brand loyalty.

> *Understanding sensory logic can help marketers fully manage consumers' experiences.*

In this book, I'll explode the rational approach to marketing and research, revealing the latest scientific findings on cognition and communication and explaining how this information can help you tap into consumers' desires and needs. The first chapters are devoted to explaining how scientists now believe our brains work and why many marketing paradigms are out of sync with these theories. In Chapter 1, I elaborate on the power of marketing that appeals to consumers' emotions, offering a justification for why this approach is ideal for our harried times, and why it makes sense in terms of our evolution. I explain in Chapter 2 how cognition and communication actually work. I end the chapter with a top 10 list that provides a general overview of how to enact sensory and emotive-based marketing. In Chapter 3, I apply these scientific findings to different marketing media, showing how companies have tapped into consumers' true feelings and desires.

In Chapter 4, I look at new ways to conduct marketing research that will tap into consumers' hearts and minds. I include a top 10 list for significantly improving research. In Chapter 5, I examine branding, showing how to translate evolutionary needs and desires into a compelling and lasting brand story. I follow with Chapter 6, which discusses how to design and execute this story.

Chapter 7 is about positioning your products so that they will resonate with consumers' innate needs and desires. In Chapter 8, I explain how different sensory and emotional clues elicit reactions, and show how to use this knowledge to attract consumers. Chapter 9 offers a final look at humans' innate desires and how to tap into them with emotive scripts. Finally, in Chapter 10, I close with a look into the future, revealing the latest scientific findings on how humans think and feel.

Throughout the book, I distill complex scientific concepts into lessons that you can use immediately as a marketer. I explain how consumers actually think and behave and discuss how marketing campaigns from my clients and leading companies have discovered powerful ways for communicating with consumers.

These ideas are the path to a new marketing paradigm. My goal in writing is to enable you to enjoy and profit from the scientific revolution now unfolding.

Notes

1. George Lakoff and Mark Johnson, *Philosophy in the Flesh: The Embodied Mind and Its Challenge to Western Thought* (New York: Basic Books, 1999), 13.

2. Gerald Zaltman and Robin Higie Coulter, "Seeing the Voice of the Customer: Metaphor-Based Advertising Research," *Journal of Advertising Research* 35, no. 4 (July/August 1995): 37.

3. Daniel Goleman, *Emotional Intelligence: Why It Can Matter More Than IQ* (New York: Bantam, 1995), 97.

4. Gerald Zaltman, "Metaphorically Speaking," *Marketing Research* 8, no. 2 (1996): 13.

5. David B. Wolfe, "What Your Customers Can't Say," *American Demographics* (February 1998): 24–29.

Fighting the Battle

How to Make the Case for the New Marketing Paradigm

Marketing departments have a huge problem. (By "marketing," I also mean advertising, sales, and other departments involved in consumer outreach or contact either within the company or as a vendor.)

A problem for all marketers is the need to provide proof that what they do actually matters and advances the company's fortunes.

Look at the situation from the chief executive officer's (CEO's) point of view. He or she has only so many resources, and stockholders to reassure and pacify. The CEO wants return on investment of significant dollars, which is critical to protect and enhance the value of the company. That's fair enough. It's up to you to get the CEO the needed information.

Remember retail guru John Wannamaker's classic nineteenth-century lament that he knew that half his advertising money was wasted, but he didn't know which half? Today, we have Lee Clow, TBWA/Chiat/Day's creator of the legendary "1984" commercial for Apple Computers, upping the ante. He contends that 90 percent of advertising has always been terrible.[1]

Why shouldn't the CEO be worried? Why shouldn't the CEO be hesitant about spending lots of cash on marketing that may not be helping the company?

As Ken Kaess, CEO of DDB Worldwide, pointed out to his colleagues when he was the incoming chairman of the American Association of Advertising Agencies, there's a need for a new way to quantify the effectiveness of advertising. He wanted something far and above the status quo client copy testing often so anachronistic that it "would almost be hilarious if it weren't still being employed by the people who actually make brand and advertising decisions based on the results."[2]

The proof that vivid sensory stimuli can make a difference is evident everywhere. For example, I was six years old when my father's job took our family to Italy. Landing in Naples on our way to Genoa, near the port area during shore leave, I saw a baby octopus hanging from a meat hook. Right then, I knew I was in a new world.

The change caught me by surprise. The new "old" world snuck up on me. I was jarred by my senses, and they followed their own logic.

Every CEO needs an equally strong experience, something to convince or remind him or her that a great skill at reading numbers and developing strategies must not blind a person to the value of making a sensory-emotive as well as rational connection with consumers.

In this chapter, I provide the justification for why the new marketing paradigms matter—because they connect companies to consumers more intimately—and I show how appealing to consumers' senses makes marketing plans far more effective.

CEOs can be reluctant to listen to projected benefits, but in my experience, they will listen to science and how scientific findings can be relevant to business, as I will explain. I'll start with why the new scientific understanding of how our senses work is especially important in today's hectic, overstimulated world. I'll show how the senses offer an immediate inroad to consumers' hearts and minds.

The Role of the Senses in Our Era

Should you want one simple reason why consumers' sensory responses matter so much to business today, look no further than the role of television. TV's emergence during the 1950s has threatened the supremacy of the written word for the first time since the invention of the printing press in the fifteenth century.[3]

Say goodbye to the rational age; it is now buried beneath entertainment and its half-sibling, infotainment. The average citizen in the developed world now watches TV for three to four hours a day. As a result, there's been a fundamental shift regarding how we receive information; to an ever-increasing degree, we're now living in a visual, postliterate society.

Why do we watch so much TV? Surely, much of the reason we want entertaining diversion is that we're burned out, starved for fun, and physically exhausted. We're overloaded, and we're seeking a way out. We want visual stimulation, and we also respond to other sensory information that breaks through the clutter.

Companies must recognize that although consumers may appear to tune out certain amounts of sensory data, they still fundamentally crave stimulation. In addition, sensory stimulation and escapism can go hand in hand, as I'll explain shortly.

Companies able to appeal to consumers' perceptual processes are in touch with the era we inhabit.

Breaking through the clutter is a cliché that nobody in marketing can escape. It's a well-known fact that people now typically experience over three thousand advertising messages daily.[4]

I've found that the key to winning over consumers is to get on their sensory bandwidth. Part of the reason senses are so powerful is because they offer instant gratification. However, companies miss the sensory mark all the time.

Consumers won't be able to tell you which ads will or will not work, but they can feel it. For example, at my company, Sensory Logic, we test consumer reactions to multiple stimuli. We line up various related advertising pieces and evaluate how people react on a gut level. Sometimes we compare competitive brands, like jeans from the Gap versus those from Levi's. We also compare different versions of ads for client companies. In one case, we lined up a pair of TV spots, a 30-second version versus a 60-second effort for the same product.

We found that the 60-second spot soon grew tiresome to viewers. In contrast, the 30-second spot captivated viewers for about 20 seconds. Our findings were confirmed by the testing and also at a pitch meeting.

I was once in the office of an executive for a potential client. A computer repairman was there, too, trying to get the executive's desktop functional again.

I started to play the 30-second spot. The commercial was running on top of the screen, with the second-by-second biofeedback scores unfolding below it. There came a point when the main actor left the scene. By then the music track was growing stale, and the actor had his back to the viewing audience. (Ask yourself: How often does seeing people turn their back to you generate warm feelings? Rarely.)

Just then—as the scores were beginning to tumble—the repair guy cut in. "I know that commercial," he said.

The executive and I looked at him, across the room. "Yeah, I know that commercial," the repairman repeated, before adding, "And at first I like it. But then it starts to annoy me."

The executive looked back down at the screen, then at me. The biofeedback verified that the commercial took a definite downturn after a promising beginning. "You guys are good," he said, smiling and nodding.

The lesson is the following: Imagery that appeals to our senses has a powerful effect on consumers, and it can lead to an emotional reaction. Although they may not be able to articulate the reasons why one ad appeals to them more than another, they nevertheless make split-second decisions based on sensory input.

Imagery processing is like microwave cooking. The brain cooks the equivalent of ready-made meals. In other words, the senses cause us to have an immediate reaction to stimuli.

I'll discuss these concepts in further detail in the next chapter. In addition, appealing to consumers' senses is the right strategy for our harried times. For example, cell phone companies besiege us with complicated monthly plans, whereas Apple Computers gives us simple "Think different" advertising, a single strong image, and plenty of white space that lets us catch our mental breath rather than encouraging us to flee.

There is no better way to generate clutter-busting impact (and appeal, too) than by creating vivid, immediate sensory stimulation. Companies that can provide adaptable, flexible, responsive interactivity will succeed in this environment.

To be successful at stimulating sensations within your customer is really the ultimate in customized relationship marketing. It's also a reminder that the senses can provide a "wow." Our media-driven society has made consumers accustomed to high production values. They're aware of such a wealth of product choices that they now fully expect to be wowed.

Leveraging the sensory bandwidth can help you avoid or get out of the commodity trap by offering your customers extra, unexpected value. Think of OXO GoodGrips kitchen utensils, which have grown market share by adding a component of visual and tactile delight to tools that otherwise serve a functional utility. With their oversized, supple handles and bright colors, these products appeal to consumers' senses and come across as fun and different, as well as easier to use by everyone, including especially people suffering from arthritis.

Forget about people's consciousness; more than articulated needs must be met. As science shows us, what's verbally known and shared is only the tip of the iceberg.

An offer that delights the senses is less likely to be passed over. It establishes a greater value that you can price accordingly to enhance profit margins—something your CEO will love.

The Senses Are Tangible and They Provide Information

The second strategic reason why the senses matter so much to business is that they build trust. They capture information that lets us make the case for why we respect or choose one company over another. To understand how we handle our investigations, think of the old *Columbo* detective episodes. Peter Falk shows up in his battered, barely running car, wearing an old, stained raincoat, and figures out what nobody else can apparently see.

How did he do it? Usually by noticing the small but crucial sensory clues that went unnoticed by the regular cops. It wouldn't occur to them to crouch down to find the subtle, telltale sign that would belie the accepted theory about who committed the crime.

Columbo's instincts are relevant because they illustrate the second strategic reason why the senses matter so much to business. Whether on purpose or by chance, companies inevitably disclose a multitude of sensory clues to consumers. For consumers, these clues are a weathervane or a barometer; in other words, they provide a way to gauge the situation. They can be felt by the consumer on either a conscious or an unconscious level. Regardless of how consumers register them, these clues either build or erode the trust on which brand equity relies.

Like good detectives, we assemble sensory impressions that give us information about our surroundings. Sight, sound, touch, taste, and smell: Where would we be without them? Sayings like "seeing is believing," "listen up," and "follow your nose" reflect society's beliefs in the power of the senses. Our sensory clues give us an idea about which companies care about us. The senses provide touch points with consumers, and they represent consumers' most innate means of judging the situations they encounter.

Today more than ever before, we live in a world of "spin," which is often politically motivated distortions of the basic facts. Although sensory data can also be manipulated, it is generally easier to be disingenuous with abstract, verbal information. We rely on our senses to "sniff out the situation" and determine who's trustworthy.

The sensory clues that both delight and reassure offer the ideal means of solving the case of long-lost customer loyalty.

The Senses Are Universal

The third and final strategic reason why the senses matter so much to business is because they help us reach across borders in an age of globalism. With globalization, tapping into international commerce has become more of a priority for many brands, and clearly there are enormous opportunities available. Of course, responding to the call for globalization can be a challenge, and reaching the world economy also means multiple markets that have multiple languages and potentially a host of communication barriers.

Fortunately, the language of the senses is nonverbal, and when used effectively, sensory marketing can transcend the inherent gaps between diverse target audiences.

Sensory marketing on an international scale also creates the following benefits:

• *Internationally*. Visual and other sensory clues provide an easy, quick way to differentiate your offer while simplifying the consumer's decision-making process. Many large brands have now taken on the status of cultural icon, reaching across borders. Do Tokyo consumers know anything about colonels or where Kentucky is located? Probably not. But they know Colonel Sanders's bow tie because KFC is a major chain in Japan.

Companies able to identify and understand the sensory clues that suit us as a species can hope to span continents by tapping into psychological truths. Ruggedness? Youth? Mobility? In overseas markets, Levi's epitomizes America's promise to let you shape your own life. I discuss these universal emotional desires in Chapter 5, which examines tapping into consumers' innate desires.

• *Domestically*. America's recent large-scale immigration doesn't always lead to the kind of melting pot assimilation that took place during earlier waves of immigration. These days, a "salad bowl" analogy is often more appropriate, because many nationalities have retained their own cultural traditions within the larger American community. Without sensory clues, today's more fractured ethnic markets are not always easy for major corporations to reach. Sensory clues can overcome communication barriers.

To return to the international benefits, my company's testing in Europe and Asia has revealed cultural subtleties. To draw some generalizations, the French are concerned with beauty, and the Germans focus on integrity. The English seem to gravitate toward marketing efforts that reflect deference, whereas the Japanese seek appropriateness.

However, if we look at the international products that work, many offer sensory gratification that transcends cultural barriers. Consider, for example, the universal appeal of Hollywood blockbuster movies. Entertainment in all of its forms now represents one of America's largest, most successful export categories; action films, in which the words are secondary, often lead the way.[5] The sensory information and visual stimulation available in these films gives them a profound universal appeal. The adrenaline rush they elicit through their powerful use of visual effects also contributes to this universal appeal.

The Senses Rule the Decision-Making Processes

So far in this chapter, I've focused on the senses from a scientific and a strategic marketing perspective, showing how to justify sensory marketing to even the most skeptical CEO. However, the CEO might need a final push to be convinced, and in this final section and in the next chapter about cognition and communication, I offer some more hard, sustained evidence from the field. I'll show how a company can conceptualize, build, and conduct its daily business around a more intuitive, sensory approach.

The latest scientific information suggests that the consumer decision-making process originates in sensory impressions. Thus, a company's ability to enhance the frequency and quality of those impressions becomes the engine that drives profitability.

The old understanding about how consumers think was grounded in the belief that people make decisions on a conscious level. It started with need recognition and then passed to the gathering of information and the evaluation of alternatives. This model saw decision making as a mechanical, even predictable, process.[6]

The truth is that we don't buy a car by reading a manual about its engine. We kick the tires, sit behind the wheel, and go for a test drive. Trying to generate consideration through information is contrary to the spirit of the age, with our desire for sensory stimulation. It also runs against human nature. Today the value proposition is more intimate and intuitive. In fact, a product's value isn't defined in the marketplace or on behalf of consumers. Instead, value is defined within consumers, through their unconscious reaction to a company's offer.

It was an artistic businessman who led the way in transforming this reality into gold.

The Sensory Magic of Walt Disney

Long before science got there, Walt Disney had already instinctively grasped the importance of replacing Descartes's "I think, therefore I am" with "I sense, therefore I am" as a means of attracting customers.

Walt began his career as a cartoonist. When he began to make animated films, he found new ways to expand the sensory bandwidth of visual images. As he pioneered the art of making cartoon films, he combined these visual images with innovations involving synchronized sound, color, three-dimensional backgrounds, and stereophonic sound.[7] His goal was to give moviegoers the richest possible sensory experience, and he was able to achieve this through his movies.

But, with film Walt still found himself inherently limited to the senses of sight and sound. So when it came time to create Disneyland, he again pushed the limits by building the first of his theme parks on an even more complete sensory basis. In effect planned as a choreographed walk-through movie, this Disney theme park engages consumers through all five of the senses.

Inside the gates, guests experience Walt's scene-by-scene script. As they funnel through Main Street U.S.A. to the other areas, the

Figure 1.1 Long before science could validate his approach, Walt Disney understood the power of both the face and smiling. Mickey Mouse reflects Darwin's realization of links between humans and animals and that an oversized head with a big smile will draw people in. (Photo courtesy of Disney Enterprises, Inc. © Disney Enterterprises, Inc.)

sensory signals they receive appear spontaneous. In fact, all of these triggers are carefully rehearsed, and they are plentiful. The Disneyland experience is like a living movie, with carefully designed sets (buildings), highly trained cast members (employees), and costumes (see Figure 1.1). Their scripts (words) and their stage movements (actions) are all rehearsed, but they appear fresh and spontaneous. Surely the most gripping aspect of this cinematic experience is the rides, some of which were planned in tight scenarios to be experienced in theater-like darkness.

How on target was Walt? His instincts were good enough that his second park, Walt Disney World Resort, qualifies as the leading tourist destination on the planet. What the parks gave him was a venue for getting closer to his customers and maximizing the sense of playful interaction that we see in his films. In contrast to a movie theater, inside the Magic Kingdom, the experience is richer and of greater duration; therefore, it leads to powerful, even lifelong connections with consumers. Only now has the business world begun to catch up with Walt Disney's vision. His innovative ideas led the way by focusing on the customer's complete experience, starting with the crucial sensory realm.

Reason versus Passion

If there is any place where the cliché about the need to "think with your head, not with your heart" has advocates, it is probably in the corner offices of strategically oriented CEOs.

The new scientific discoveries about how people make decisions should change how they feel about reason and passion—because the verdict from the scientific community is in favor of passion.

I believe that most CEOs want to think of their customers as rational beings. This prevailing bias must change for companies to connect with customers on a deeper, more meaningful level. The payoff isn't just to make the marketing folks happy—it gets back to why a company is in business in the first place, to make money. In the end, sensory marketing is the key to financial success, rewarding both shareholders and employees. The payoff for winning customer loyalty is lucrative.

Remember, people decide emotionally, and I don't just mean the sensitive types who follow their hearts. Everyone does this. In the end, sensory marketing matters because it facilitates and locks into place an emotional connection between a company and consumers, a connection that until formed, prevents a new product from succeeding in the marketplace. In the next chapter, I'll show exactly how the brain works, and how sensory data is the doorway into consumers' minds and hearts.

In summary, the main points in this chapter are as follows:

- Business today is oriented to a model of the consumer as a rational decision maker. In the next chapter, I'll explain the latest scientific understanding of how we actually make up our minds.

- Sensory marketing is a crucial tool that bridges cultural and international barriers. The senses are universal, and appealing to them through marketing efforts represents a potent method for tapping into the global marketplace.

- We unconsciously gather information about our surroundings through our senses. They paint a picture of our surroundings for us and guide us in our decision-making processes.

- Consumers process sensory information instantaneously, giving sensory marketing an immediacy that's lacking in methods that treat consumers as purely rational beings.

- Sensory marketing also appeals to domestic consumers because, again, the senses are universal. This type of marketing approach is perfect for harried, overstimulated consumers. In spite of their apparent elusiveness, appealing to their senses cuts through other stimuli and captures their attention.

Now that we've established the value of marketing to the senses, I turn to the second stage of the consumer decision-making process: emotional assessment.

Notes

1. Lee Clow, quoted in Christine Canabou, "Advertising Under Review," *Fast Company* (April 2002): 62.

2. Ken Kaess, quoted in Stan Rapp, "Something New under the Advertising Sun," *DMA Insider* (Fall 2002): 10.

3. Neil Postman, *Amusing Ourselves to Death* (New York: Viking, 1985).

4. David Schenk, *Data Smog: Surviving the Information Glut* (San Francisco: Harper, 1997), 27.

5. Benjamin R. Barber, *Jihad vs. McWorld: Terrorism's Challenge to Democracy* (New York: Ballantine, 1995), 307–309.

6. Philip Kotler, *Marketing Management: Analysis, Planning, Implementation, and Control*, 8th ed. (Englewood Cliffs, NJ: Prentice Hall, 1994), 193–198.

7. B. Joseph Pine II and James H. Gilmore, *The Experience Economy: Work Is Theatre & Every Business a Stage* (Boston: Harvard Business School Press, 1999), 2.

Rationality Redefined

How Cognition and Communication Actually Work

When scientists announced in June 2000 they had developed a rough draft of the human genetic code, everyone sat up and took notice. This was big news. We now had a basic instruction manual for the inner machinery of every member of our species. The *Los Angeles Times* compared the discovery to Lewis and Clark's mapping of the Northwest Territories.[1]

Others went even further. The editors of the British science journal *Nature* embossed their cover with one of Western civilization's most notable symbols of life and creation—the part of Michelangelo's Sistine Chapel fresco that shows the outstretched hand of God reaching toward Adam's hand. If anyone had doubts about whether the twenty-first century would usher in the era of biotechnology, those reservations must have immediately evaporated on the news of this medical milestone.

There's also another, quieter revolution in biotechnology that applies as much to business as to medicine—a growing understanding of how the human brain works. Few people have grasped the power of its implications. In fact, new scientific insights suggest that much of human nature is hardwired through evolution in a way that relates directly to sensory logic.

How the Brain Works

The lesson from science is that our decision-making process isn't really under our control—the way we think and make decisions is ingrained in our species. (As I'll explain later, this unconscious mode of decision making also relates to our inability to voice how we feel about products.) Therefore, business models that assume a conscious, rational purchase decision-making model are faulty.

In effect, Mercedes-Benz can run all the advertising it wants championing the automaker's superior German engineering, but is there any doubt that the hook lies in its emotional, non-rational, ego-affirming appeal? The same holds true for Rolex, whose watches signal success. Both of these companies might run print ads touting the craftsmanship of their products, but when you meet a true devotee of these brands, you understand that their affection is much more emotional than rational. The emotional affirmation provided by these products feels good enough that few of us would ever attempt to validate this buzz with facts.

The scientific results from tracing the brain's circuitry are in line with how companies like Rolex and Mercedes-Benz actually approach the consumer decision-making model. But as I pointed out in the last chapter, most companies still operate under an older assumption. They subscribe to the widely accepted idea that the buyer passes through three stages: cognitive, affective, and behavioral. In other words, we learn, feel, and do (see Figure 2.1).

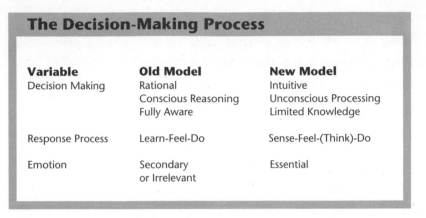

The Decision-Making Process

Variable	Old Model	New Model
Decision Making	Rational	Intuitive
	Conscious Reasoning	Unconscious Processing
	Fully Aware	Limited Knowledge
Response Process	Learn-Feel-Do	Sense-Feel-(Think)-Do
Emotion	Secondary	Essential
	or Irrelevant	

Figure 2.1 The Decision-Making Process

Two variables exist that sometimes alter the older understanding of cognition: the amount of involvement a product category creates for consumers and the degree of differentiation a company achieves. Those variables may cause the learn-feel-do sequence to shift a little, but in the old model, feeling never leads, and learning is most often in first place.[2]

The new model poses as profound a change as Copernicus's discovery that the sun—not the Earth—was the center of the universe. In a move that challenges the past 300 years of Western thought, scientists have downgraded the importance of our conscious, rational thoughts. Instead, they argue that our largely unconscious, sensory-emotive reactions shape everything—how we relate to companies, how we interpret advertising, and how we respond to both products and services, among other things.[3]

A sense-feel-(think)-do model is, in short, more accurate.

In the new understanding of cognition, the body and mind aren't really separate from one another. Instead, scientists now believe that the mind dwells in the body, and reason is shaped by what the senses take in and how the body functions.[4] This intimate interplay means that we're really "mind/body" people. It also means that advances in science have effectively given us a new kind of consumer.

Companies must take heed of the following lessons from science:

- Human senses are the most effective information-gathering system ever invented. They absorb our experiences or take-away impressions of a company and its offer(s) and, in the process, influence how our minds respond.

- Despite what rationalists theorize, we're not machines; we're animals, linked by traits shared across the species. Our conceptual systems draw on the same common physical realm—the world around us. There is a profound universality to people's reactions that extends to acting on instincts formed throughout the history of humanity. Our collective unconscious is like a template for the entire species. The template will enable astute companies to build marketing platforms that can still be effective and cost-efficient in an era of globalization. (I discuss this template in further detail beginning in Chapter 5.)

- Access to what is in your customers' heads requires an understanding of what is happening in-

(continued)

side their bodies. The process people enact in forming their reactions and engaging in purchase behavior isn't based on rational criteria alone. It mostly happens on a more intuitive, gut level. This process is hard to express, and it's even harder to quantify feelings that may originate in a seemingly vague factor like the new car smell that tells you "new is nice."

The Ground Truth

To draw an analogy from real life, the U.S. Air Force no longer relies on pilots' estimation of whether they have hit their intended targets, as they once did. They now recognize that this reliance on aerial estimations was leading to sometimes vastly inflated reports of success. Everyone was suddenly Eddie Rickenbacker, the World War I ace pilot.

Instead, the air force now has spotters on the ground who can report the truth about whether the objective was realized. Business needs to employ a similar mechanism.

The air-to-ground difference is like the mind/body split. We consciously think we know what's happening when we make decisions, but our body knows the truth.

That's why I have customized research tools able to explore and bridge the gap. I will discuss the tools in greater length later in this book. What you need to know for now is this:

Tools, such as biofeedback, let us read the body's reaction to marketing stimuli through objective, real-time measurements.

The value of using such tools is that they enable marketers to see what products and offers break through the clutter. Biofeedback relies on the body's natural electricity to gauge arousal and the likability that drives consumer preferences. Besides measuring sweat gland activity, this tool uses sensors to detect smile or frown muscle activity, and the resulting insights show exactly how consumers feel. I'll discuss this mechanism in greater detail in Chapter 4, which covers research methods.

To use an example about the power of biofeedback from my company's history, my second client was U-Haul. Its CEO felt that the company's signage didn't "pop" as well as their competitors'. Our task was to find out whether this was the case for consumers, and then to verify which of the new signage options would win among consumers.

We first tried traditional questions and answers to see which sign would win for interest and appeal. This approach didn't help—it led to three possibilities, including the eventual winner, bunched together as data points on a graph of results. We needed a tool that would more clearly spell out which sign would prevail among consumers.

We used biofeedback to assess the situation more clearly. Biofeedback is a superior tool for helping gauge the body's first reaction. We wanted to see what sign truly had curbside appeal—after all, that's what dealer signage is all about. The outcome was that the CEO's gut instinct was right. The competitor's signage sat up in the preference zone: high impact and high appeal. U-Haul's clunky old signage was dead on arrival—flat on impact with negative appeal.

After biofeedback testing, we went back to the drawing board. The resulting signage proved so strong that in later biofeedback testing it matched up with the competition head to head. We were able to create a new look and feel that was incredibly effective.

With questions and answers, the choice might have gone to either signage showing the rental trucks or signage emphasizing price. With biofeedback testing, it became clear that the first of those options really wasn't appealing to consumers on a gut level. Meanwhile, with biofeedback data, the pricing signage tanked. The winner was new signage that shows a visual of a curving, looming open road. This image holds the promise of adventure. It's all-American, like Huckleberry Finn lighting out for parts unknown. In retrospect, perhaps it was an obvious choice, except that conventional testing had at best a one-in-three shot of getting it right.

As to the consumer response, dealers reported favorable customer comments and increased sales. For example, one said, "The amazing thing is that, despite being in this location for 12 years, the new sign is bringing in customers who say they never knew we were here."[5]

The U-Haul story confirms what science has found, including the following:

- The signage with the most compelling image, the open road, proved to be dominant, and the reason related to the fact that we think by using our senses to guide us—they take in far more information than we can knowingly process. Human reasoning isn't only abstract and objective; a sign that provides an intriguing visual attracts us because our reaction process starts with sensory perceptions.

- Based on the results of the questions and answers (which is of course based on a conscious, more ra-

(continued)

tional approach to cognition), the signage with the pricing seemed like a viable option. In biofeedback, the vista of an open road was the clear winner. Indeed, going to cost was a dead-end, and it set up the chance for consumers to start worrying about terms and conditions, the contract, and other hassles. It forced a rational response, in exchange for bypassing the possibility of forging an emotional connection. In contrast, the open road sign transformed U-Haul in consumers' minds. The company no longer appeared as a cold entity set on earning money while you endure the agony of moving your possessions yourself. Instead, U-Haul emerged more as a friend helping you explore the next big adventure in your life. It represented freedom and possibility.

A few of the target audience members, our 20-something participants in the study, could articulate these points. Most couldn't (or didn't bother to do so), but by scientifically quantifying their initial gut reactions, the immediate sensory biofeedback readings told the story for them.

1-2-3 Brains in All

Let's turn now to how our brains work. As I've said, decision making is far more instantaneous than we'd imagined in the past. I'm reminded of how our brains actually work whenever I play sports. I'm no sports superstar, but every now and then in basketball or tennis, I will make an incredible shot I usually can't make. It happens almost without any conscious effort on my part—as if I'm just a bystander, only realizing after the fact what I've done.

In the marketplace, consumers react instinctively, too. Companies need to realize, accept, and leverage the fact that most of their marketing messages are received on a level the target audience isn't even aware of.

The U-Haul case isn't an isolated example. The human body will respond or not respond to sensory clues as it sees fit. More often than not, conscious, rational, attitudinal reactions are overshadowed by emotional responses.

To understand how things work, let's start with a question: How strong is the mind–body link? Scientists have recently come up with the startling conclusion that without smell—the first of our senses—we wouldn't have developed a brain at all. Only after a small lump of olfactory tissue atop the nerve cord grew into a brain did the early, reptilian version of humanity literally get off the ground and start to become the species we are today.[6]

In effect, cognition evolved due to our ability to smell. Sight only became dominant once we were upright, walking, above the ground, looking around for our next meal.

The brain didn't just spontaneously appear as the complex organ that it is. It evolved from a much simpler structure. It isn't enough to know about the lateralism concept of left- versus right-brain thinking that earned a Nobel Prize for Roger Sperry in the 1960s. (His research found that left-brained people are logical and linear, whereas right-brained people are visually oriented and the touchy-feel types.[7]) The new scientific understanding holds that the brain is made up of components from different eras of evolution that interact with each other in fascinating ways.

Over a decade ago, Paul MacLean found that there are actually three brains at work inside us.[8] In simplified terms, these three brains consist of:

- The original brain, smallest in size and dating back to our earliest stages of evolution, is the lizard (reptilian) brain. Its purpose is to maintain basic survival functions, such as respiration, digestion, circulation, and reproduction. Think of it as the janitor in the basement of the brain, taking care of the basics to keep the building running.

- Next in both size and evolution is the leopard (early mammalian) brain, which wraps around the lizard brain. This middle brain adds the capacity for emotion and coordination of movement. This is where we take in the information from our senses. Imagine this brain as the doorman on the ground floor of the building. A role of the middle brain is to let in what it (often unconsciously) deems to be important. Once inside, the stimuli get ushered into the brain's emotional hot spot. What reaction it gets there colors and even determines the reaction of the brain upstairs, the learning brain.

(continued)

- Our largest and most recently evolved brain is the learning (late mammalian) brain. The cerebral cortex provides the ability to solve problems, use language and numbers, develop memory, and be creative. This brain is like the CEO on the top floor of the building. This brain makes our rational, cerebral decisions. See Figure 2.2 for an illustration of these three types of brain.

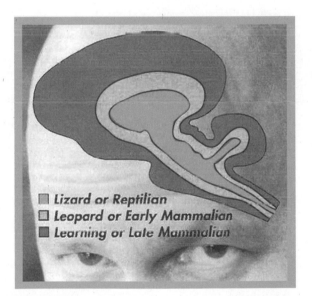

Figure 2.2 Size doesn't always matter. Our "middle," leopard brain came second in evolution, adding the fight-or-flight response, and exerts a strong influence on the larger, rationally oriented learning brain that came last in evolution. (Adapted with permission from Pierce J. Howard, *Owner's Manual for the Brain* [Atlanta: Bard Press, 2000], p. 38.)

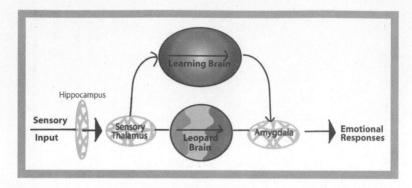

Figure 2.3 The straight, low-road "emotional" path for decision making is quicker but dirtier, less precise. It colors our perceptions prior to conscious thought. However, even the high-road, "rational" path for decision making loops back to the amygdala, the brain's emotional thermometer. (Adapted with permission of Simon & Schuster Adult Publishing Group from *The Emotional Brain* by Joseph LeDoux, Copyright © 1996 by Joseph LeDoux, p. 164.)

Clearly, the old model of rational thought emphasizes the learning brain. The newfound reality is that the leopard brain is crucial. For marketers, this middle brain is important because it helps shape how consumers process marketing stimuli and arrive at purchase decisions (see Figure 2.3).

Indeed, the learning brain desperately needs the leopard brain. Think of it as a company president who never comes out of his office to walk the factory floor. The learning brain is completely out of touch on its own, and it has considerable blind spots. It lives in the abstract, in theories, hypothetical situations, and generalizations.

Specific sensory details and perceptual facts are what the brain thrives on. Our language and quantitative and reasoning skills—the domain of the learning brain—came later in evolution and are weaker. As Gerald Zaltman observed in the *Journal of Advertising Research*, "Verbal language developed only recently in the context of human evolution and written language developed even more recently. Thus, the human brain did not evolve to favor verbal functions."[9]

Moreover, not only is our brain relatively new at language skills and rational thought, today these skills are receding as we become more and more reliant on multimedia stimulation.

For marketers, this understanding of cognition explains why certain brands attract life-long devotees. Consumers, such as Harley-Davidson's loyal bikers, blow past the fact that there are better, less expensive motorcycles for sale because the tribal culture of riding a hog stimulates their senses and captures their hearts.

Meanwhile, most of the business world continues to focus more on the largest, rationally oriented brain. (Furthermore, as I'll discuss in the next chapter, much of marketing research relies on the idea that people can effectively articulate how they're feeling about a brand or an offer.)

The opportunity for competitive advantage lies in getting in tune with the leopard brain's sensory-emotive mind–body connection.

Our Perceptual Systems

To complete the picture of how the sensory realm works for consumers, there is one more step. Until recently, the prevailing scientific consensus was that the newer—larger—learning brain

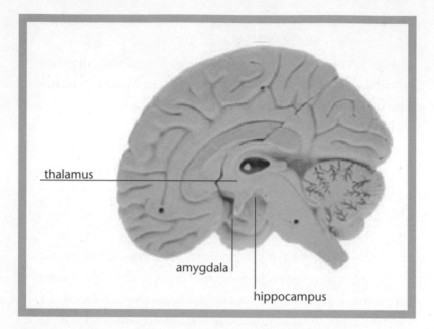

Figure 2.4 Whether marketers know it or not, the brain really does have a "hot button." In fact, it has two of them: The amygdala consists of a pair of almond-sized entities.

controlled and drove our everyday mental activity. The idea that brain size matters was one that most scientists took for granted. They saw the mind as operating abstractly from the senses, all but removed from the influence of sensory perceptions.

The new emerging scientific consensus today is almost entirely changed. What made the difference? The leopard brain and its trio of key players:[10] the hippocampus, the amygdala, and the thalamus (see Figure 2.4). These are hardly household names, but together they're the biological trigger system that makes it possible—even financially imperative—to create a sensory-emotive connection with consumers.

Let's focus for now on the sensory players: The hippocampus primarily, and then also in passing our sensory-relay mechanism (the thalamus).

The hippocampus is vital. It's the screen door to a person's psyche. It lets in what it deems to be shocking, novel, emotionally significant, or networked to the familiar. Therefore, successful marketing seduces the hippocampus.

It's that basic. Perceptual awareness depends on the hippocampus to filter incoming sensory data from print ads to products. The hippocampus is a natural organizer. Because our senses take in far more than we can handle, the hippocampus has its work cut out for it. Below the radar screen of conscious awareness, it determines what stimuli will grab a mental foothold. What doesn't make the cut never gets sent along by the thalamus to acquire either an emotional or conscious, rational response.

Companies must realize that most of their marketing messages are received on a unconscious level by the target audience. Furthermore, the hippocampus's receptivity will make or break the chance to score big in the marketplace.

I conclude this chapter with an overview of what the new understanding about cognition means to marketers on a daily basis, and how to win over the hippocampus. In the next chapter, I look at marketing applications within each specific medium available to marketers and advertisers.

Top 10 Rules for Marketing to the Senses

1. Keep It Simple

At first glance, this might seem to be only a sensory rule. But ultimately, the goal of creating clues that are easily followed is an emotional issue involving comfort or a lack thereof. Here's why:

> Sensory clues that are more readily grasped are more fun and make us feel better. In summary, complexity runs counter to the wisdom of evolution.

For instance, we see a bottle of Heinz ketchup, and it becomes both literally and figuratively comfort food. In an ever more fragmented world, it provides, on a functional level, simple information processing. At the same time, emotionally it constructs an internal signpost that takes us back to childhood. At ease, we don't feel a need to question or analyze—we already trust. Without needing to scrutinize it, we register the bottle's simple, classic label and race past any price point comparison to lock in the emotional connection we feel.

In contrast, clues that are physically obscure or blurry create the equivalent emotional reaction. Marketing that creates confusion in consumers is scary, uncomfortable, and quite simply dumb. As a species, we want to enter a situation and get a sense of the

(continued)

vista. A certain degree of intrigue or suspense is fine, but when there's too much subtlety and too high a degree of difficulty, our ability to form a judgment is hindered.

2. Relevancy Drives Connection

Whether we know it or not, we as consumers often walk around with a *For Sale* sign around our necks. We want to be lured. We're always looking for greater fulfillment, and a company's offer might be just the ticket. Emotions turn on because we process a sensory clue and the offer it illustrates is meaningful to us. In short, it's relevant to us.

Relevancy has to do with possibilities, the belief that whatever is now on the horizon can make a real difference in our lives. Consumers want to believe that the breakthrough beauty product will not only erase their wrinkles but make them more attractive and thereby give them a new social life.

Sparked by the chance of finding relevancy, our emotions intuitively gather more information than reason alone can provide. Rationally, the higher the cost of the product, the greater the need for utility, but on an emotional basis, relevancy often outstrips literal value and drives a different decision that feels right.

(continued)

3. Always Sell Hope

As consumers, we long for what will lift daily existence into another, higher, more enriched sphere. Such hope could perhaps be derided as fantasy or even merely as selfishness and self-indulgence, but to do so would be wrong. As evolutionary psychology reminds us, humans are driven to feel good about ourselves. Self-confidence is often inflated, but it's an evolutionary advantage to feel good because it instills in people a degree of vitality that in turn attracts allies and friends.

There are, however, two important corollaries to this rule. The first is that although a company must always sell hope, it may do so by peddling fear—thereby reminding us of what we hope to avoid. The second corollary is that whereas a company must always sell hope, it must deliver on faithful security.

The truth is that nothing deceives more cruelly than false hope. The payback? Consumers will mercilessly punish a company if its marketing efforts make a promise on which the company underdelivers.

4. Believability Sticks

Trust is a critical element in business, but it's also incredibly fragile. It's difficult to gain and easy to lose. With trust, there is no slow demise—it crashes. As

(continued)

the case with Firestone involving the defective tires on SUVs proved, when a company loses consumer trust, a death spiral commences that no rational, utilitarian, product-oriented marketing campaign can hope to stop.

The reason that trust is so elusive is grounded in the fact that the whole company–consumer relationship lies beyond reason—it's deeper and more emotionally based. Why is trust so important to a company? Because if a company can embed its touch points with sensory clues that signal (but don't exaggeratedly scream) empathy, the company can come out ahead. Trust is important to consumers because we want to believe, want to belong, and want to feel intimately attached to what we perceive as an ally.

We guard against a fundamental lack of believability that our gut instincts tell us "smells" like danger, and we discount the value of anything we don't trust.

5. Make It Memorable

Consumers are not abstract thinkers, so a company must root its pitch in the senses. Have a focal point, and be easy to perceive. To survive the initial sensory screening—without which no memory is possible—a company is wise to adhere to the hierarchy of sensory intake whereby visual imagery and then the other

(*continued*)

four senses are likely to predominate over interest in the written word. In that way, a greater, deeper involvement with consumers becomes possible.

To avoid being forgettable, sensory clues can secure a more permanent status in our lives by one of two routes.

These clues must burn bright, and they must hit an emotional hot button. We're naturally most attuned to what's distinct, novel, and involves change while also being significant and relevant to us.

Second, companies must build a house instead of pitching a tent. In other words, a company can achieve mental stickiness by attaching clues to what is already part of our memories.

We favor coherence over arbitrariness, so whatever relates to something we already know means a company is halfway home with the consumer; repetition does the rest.

---

6. Keep It Close to Home

There are very few (if any) commercial rewards for trying to broaden the target audience's collective comfort zone beyond what is already known and familiar. The better route for a company is to entrench its offer in something that is already recog-

(continued)

nizable to that audience. Deep down, go with the known sensory clues and the fundamental patterns of life that evolutionary psychology helps illuminate. Then, closer to the surface, add in the local, customized accent points that function like spices for a meal.

The truth is that the range of what is acceptable to people is small. As consumers, we're most likely to relate to what we know best. We draw us/them dichotomies all the time, for better or for worse. For marketers, it's essential to appeal to consumers' sense of what's familiar.

> *Familiarity breeds comfort, and everyone wants to be comfortable. Thus, it's far easier to gain buy-in by never selling us something new or strange ("foreign") until and unless it's first been wrapped in the familiar.*

Once the threat of the new is removed, a company can then in effect sell consumers ourselves instead. By this I mean that a company can get us to buy products and concepts already known and accepted by us. The problem with foreign news is that we often don't have a mental map for it; we tend to dismiss it because it's not our country. Foreign news has nothing to resonate with, in contrast to local news that easily triggers the mental imagery locked in memory.

(continued)

7. *Leverage the Sensory Bandwidth*

As consumers, our sensory experiences or take-away impressions of an offer set the stage for whether we will purchase or not. However, most companies aren't thorough and systematic in their approach to leveraging the sensory bandwidth.

There are three factors that influence the perceptual process: the perceiver, the setting, and the perceived.[11] A company must pay close attention to all three if it hopes to make a connection. Consumers are the complex perceivers, often in three mental time zones at once: yesterday's sensory memories, today's split-second assigning of value based on experiences, and tomorrow's projected hopes or fears. Marketing gains in power to the extent that it can utilize all three time zones.

The second factor, the setting, should be studied because the signal-to-noise ratio or clutter of the setting in which the clues are encountered will influence their effectiveness. Finally, the third factor, the perceived, involves the specific clues that benefit from good design work that skillfully weaves together characteristics like contrast, intensity, size, and motion.

As a well-managed unit, perceiver, setting, and the perceived enable a company to create a strong intuitive connection with consumers that a consciously derived, rational response can't possibly hope to match.

(continued)

8. *Focus on Faces*

Charles Darwin himself studied faces across cultures and wrote about the universality of human emotion. Part of the explanation for why faces are so powerful to humans is without doubt pure aesthetics. A pretty or handsome face is enjoyable to observe. But there are also other reasons why the face engages us so much as a species, and why marketing should in turn include the use of faces whenever feasible.

Other reasons for the power of faces include the following.

Faces command notice because they're the place of four of our major sensory inputs: eyes, ears, nose, and mouth. A second consideration is that the face is an easy, immediate barometer by which to gauge health and vitality. Finally, we focus on faces because they're full of emotion, which is valuable information for anyone trying to read another person.

Companies need to keep in mind that showing close-ups of faces offers a great opportunity to break through the clutter because people relate to other people. Faces grab and retain our attention. In the faces of a company's models and those of the service personnel and our fellow shoppers, we look to see if

(continued)

they seem truly happy and if they are somebody with whom we can identify. A company should always remember that to lose face isn't just about humiliation. It's about robbing an offer of intimacy and losing the chance to differentiate a product by creating a powerful sensory-emotive connection.

9. Don't Lead with Price

There are three steps in the consumer decision-making process: sensory impressions, emotional assessment, and a rational confirmation. Where does price fit into the picture? As a sensory clue, a posted price in a store or print ad is an impersonal abstraction. When marketing leads with price, this indirect contact has a negative effect on how deeply the emotional assessment engages us as consumers.

Price is not in any psychological list of basic human needs. Worth is, but that's a translation that gains its power and relevance once we've actually experienced the offer. Not surprisingly, then, price lacks in either sensory or emotive linkage.

It's not that price-based marketing doesn't feel right. It just doesn't resonate at all. What leading with price does is to tell consumers to look around and compare because price is important. It turns the sale into a commodity or simply a transaction. To en-

(continued)

courage consumers to make the purchase on a cognitive, learning-brain level means losing the opportunity for the initial emotional connection. You can take consumers from the emotive to the cognitive. But you can't fully take them from cognitive to emotive. What's lost is the chance to drive past price to a more lucrative impulse purchase and the potential to forge a lasting bond with consumers that will bring them back for more.

10. Be Sensitive to the Gender Gap

This joker's wild: In marketing as in life in general, sex and humor are risky cards to play. The power of sex can't be denied—nothing else works better in terms of grabbing our attention immediately, and when it relates to the offer (as is the case with something like suntan lotion), at least the signals are swimming the same way.

Although the use of sex, bawdy humor, or anything that creates a strong sensation increases arousal, what happens in terms of emotional acceptance? Scientific studies show that on average men react to positive stimuli with both arousal and appeal, but with no arousal and a negative appeal reaction to negative stimuli. Women are the opposite in terms of how arousal works. Positive stimuli are well liked but may not engage them much. Negative stimuli create

(continued)

a strong negative reaction all around.[12] The implications for marketing, especially if led by men, is the following.

A company can get hurt because it unintentionally offends or alienates some consumers—most likely women—by using visual or other content that men find adventuresome and women find dangerous or offensive and therefore unwelcome.

Now that I've run through some ground rules for marketing with sensory logic, in Chapter 3 I turn to marketing applications for marketers within different medium.

Notes

1. Paul Jacobs and Aaron Zitner, "Scientists Reach Milestone in Mapping of Human Genome," *Los Angeles Times*, June 27, 2000, p. A1.

2. Philip Kotler, *Marketing Management: Analysis, Planning, Implementation, and Control*, 8th ed. (Englewood Cliffs, NJ: Prentice Hall, 1994), 193–198.

3. George Lakoff and Mark Johnson, *Philosophy in the Flesh: The Embodied Mind and Its Challenge to Western Thought* (New York: Basic Books, 1999), 4.

4. Anthony Damasio, *Descartes' Error: Emotion, Reason, and the Human Brain* (New York: Avon Books, 1995), 248.

5. "Light Up Your Dealerships! New Illuminated Sign Increases Rentals," *U-Haul News*, May 2000, p. 13.

6. Diane Ackerman, *A Natural History of the Senses* (New York: Vintage Books, 1990), 20.

7. Tracy Staton, "In Your Right Mind?" *American Way* (November 2000): 153; Paul A. Sperry and Roger Wolcott Sperry, *Science and Moral Priority: Merging Mind, Brain, and Human Values* (New York: Columbia University Press, 1982).

8. Paul MacLean, *The Triune Brain in Evolution: Role in Paleocerebral Functions* (New York: Plenum, 1990).

9. Gerald Zaltman and Robin Higie Coulter, "Seeing the Voice of the Customer: Metaphor-Based Advertising Research," *Journal of Advertising Research* 35, no. 4 (July/August 1995): 37.

10. Jason Zweig, "Are You Wired for Wealth?" *Money*, October 2002, 75–83.

11. John R. Schermerhorn, James G. Hunt, and Richard N. Osborn, *Organizational Behavior*, 7th ed. (New York: Wiley, 1999), 84–97.

12. Margaret M. Bradley and Peter J. Lang, "Measuring Emotion: Behavior, Feeling, and Physiology," in *Cognitive Neuroscience of Emotion*, ed. Richard D. Lane, Lynn Nadel, and Geoffrey Ahern (New York: Oxford University Press, 2000), 252–253.

CHAPTER

3

Marketing
Backed by Science

*Applying Scientific Insights for
Marketing Success*

A few months after I launched my own business, I was starting
to make a pitch to another company when the woman on
the other end of the phone cut me off by saying, "Just spit it
out. What are you trying to sell me?"

That was my last call for the day. Painful? Yes, but it also taught
me a thing or two about marketing: everything from how hard it is
to get out there in front of (potential) customers to how hard it is to
stay true to what you supposedly know. There I was, advocating the
importance of simplicity, even as my offer, brochure, and pitch were
anything but easy to take in and understand.

It's easy to forget the basics. I've created this chapter with the
goal of defining easy-to-understand, hands-on ways to reach con-

sumers in different media. The rest of the book offers more complex, nuanced plans, but in this chapter, I outline tried-and-true methods. Start to say something about any marketing medium, from promotion to product, place or the people involved, and you run the risk of generating a thin patina of truisms. At times, maybe even quite often, I'm in such danger myself. Obviously, there are always exceptions to every rule.

My way out of trouble is to move past telling you that you must always put exactly an inch of air between the photo and the caption in a print ad or other such great tricks of the trade that will make you rich. Instead, my aim is to get at the heart of each of these media outlets, to talk about it from the perspective introduced by the new scientific findings. Knowing that people's unconscious is so dominant changes the equation for how we work in each of these mediums. The same goes for the new sense-feel-(think)-do decision-making model and for how evolutionary psychology affirms the importance of security and comfort as motivational drivers, as well as for how our quick-and-dirty neurological "back alley" to the leopard brain's amygdala transforms us into largely emotional decision makers. All of these factors call for a new breed of marketing and advertising in each of the available mediums for reaching consumers.

TV Spots: The Hook Is in the Unseen

I cited it once in Chapter 1, and now I'll repeat the statistic: Two-thirds of all stimuli reaching the brain are visual. There it is—the fact that should drive how all TV advertising is conducted, all the time.

Amazingly enough, this guideline often gets ignored. It seems simple enough, but turn on your TV set, and I bet that the next wave of commercials you see will include several that don't make the medium work for them.

My company has tested numerous commercials in which the visuals aren't compelling. Not surprisingly, they don't test very well. However, those kinds of commercials keep getting made anyway.

Here are some of the generalizations I can make based on personal experience and my research involving biofeedback.

- You should be able to watch the commercial with the sound off on your TV and feel that the commercial still communicates.

- You should have a dominant visual, something that tells the story in an instant and summarizes everything.

- You should have that one dominant visual someplace that matters, like near the start or the end of the commercial, so that you increase the odds that it will get noticed.

- You should have at least a secondarily dominant visual at either the beginning or the end. Better yet, have it in both places.

- You should not give in to the idea that a string of visuals run together is an adequate substitute for the one dominant, compelling visual that can bring the viewer home.

Remember, making TV spots costs lots of money, and a lot of companies aren't well served by what they're paying for. Now I want to move on to the other big issue—time (or the lack of it) in a 30-second commercial that works like a mirage. As a species we most often focus on stimuli involving intensity and change. But as I've mentioned, creating such a blur isn't as effective as creative directors may think it is. Constant change isn't ultimately change at all—it's just some more motion wearing us down, turning more into less.

Time really is the other big consideration in making an effective TV spot. There usually isn't much of it, and your spot must make its mark instantly. Remember how the mind works—impressions happen unconsciously, and they also happen quickly.

The solution is to remember—or realize—that a good commercial doesn't have to do it all on its own. Great TV spots find the extra, hidden power in the viewer. Remember the Michelin commercials that featured a baby rolling downhill in a tire? The emphasis on a baby evokes our strongest instinctive urge to protect the species. With the tire suggestive of mother or an inner tube for floating in the lake during the summer, Michelin has imbued an otherwise seemingly innocuous product—tires—with considerable sensory-emotive power.

The successful spots set forth quick, easily accessible imagery capable of resonating with a context—associations—that already lie buried deep inside the viewer.

In advertising a pick-up truck, for instance, it's best to attach the product to an existing story—one that speaks to qualities like toughness, courage, and the great outdoors. Nowhere are the great outdoors bigger than in the West. A pick-up truck is the horse under the saddle of a cowboy or outlaw, instead of the ox under the yoke of settlers hoping to farm.

In short, a good commercial doesn't have to communicate; it can also just reference stories that we already know. For more on building an effective story and its effect on branding, turn to Chapter 10.

Radio Ads: An Intimate Conversation

Radio is advertising that talks to an audience typically engaged in doing something else at the same time, like driving. We might well be driving during rush hour, when the traffic drives us crazy and we're going to or returning home from a job we're likely to consider increasingly boring or frustrating.

In order words, watch out: Your audience isn't exactly in the mood. Yet . . . if a radio ad can get to the listener, it will be a really good connection.

Here's why. Being in your car isn't the same as being in your living room in front of the TV. It's even more personal—it's your space. Where are you when you're driving and faced with traffic, road signs, billboards, and road and weather conditions all competing for attention? You're snug behind the wheel in your own mobile pod of privacy.

The reason why radio has the potential for letting you forge a great emotional connection with the listener is that it's the ultimate one-on-one medium.

As a marketer, make the intimacy of radio work for you. Talk in the first person (I, me, mine, we, our) and make the radio ad a chat between friends. Too often companies sound distant and impersonal. Their radio ads come at us as if they're being shouted through a bullhorn from atop a building. Just because you've been reduced to a single sensory channel—sound—is no reason to panic; instead, to simulate a personal, real, intimate conversation with the audience, an ad must project and interact.

Most radio ads settle for loudness. However, there are other means of generating attention while also fostering intimacy. You and I and every vocal analyst intuitively understand that people reveal their emotions and, thereby, connect with others through the way they talk.

Forget volume, and make your listeners forget about traffic by using these other opportunities to get in close:

- **Intonation:** A rising and falling vocal pitch (in other words, vibration frequency) provides the audio clues that signal intensity and can help grab and hold attention.

- **Timing:** Different emotional states tend to be characterized by varying utterance lengths and rates of speech. The rhythm of the radio ad's script provides a chance for emotional resonance.

- **Articulation and respiration:** Emotions produce change in these two modes of expression as well, contributing to a hidden yet real emotional hum. Creating a genuine feeling frequency can allow you to connect with consumers.

Use these methods to bring listeners into the medium and transform a good radio spot from being a background distraction while driving into the foreground of interest. But any advice I could give you about creating intimacy in radio advertising would be incomplete if I didn't mention one other thing:

When radio really works, it's actually a visual medium.

If you're sitting with a friend and talking, you can envision the situation she or he is reliving. Help your listeners do likewise in hearing your ad. Take inspiration from the fact that when Orson Welles broadcast "The War of the Worlds," many people listening on their radios really thought that Martians had landed in central New Jersey, ready to conquer the Earth.

Print Ads: Long Copy Isn't Always the Best

The marketing medium in which the old rational, utilitarian bias remains most evident is print ads. Page through most publications—especially those involving computers—and you will often find long, attribute-driven copy that seeks to persuade readers that a product is superior for reasons many of us can't or wouldn't bother to discern.

This kind of print ad assumes a traditional, fully conscious, reason-based needs recognition model. It pushes us out rather than pulling us in, and in doing so it ignores the scientific insights that align psychology with behavioral economics.

Based on research studies in which psychologists use biofeedback to test patient reactions to complex formats, I argue for the 60/30/10 rule:

- For 60 percent of the readers, a print ad must work like the best of outdoor advertising—it must capitalize on a visual and a headline. It must catch them and command their attention with an image point, a brief message, and then the brand name. They won't read into the copy.

- For 30 percent of the readers, a print ad will stop them, giving marketers a chance to engage them a little more. They might read into the copy.

- 10 percent of readers are actually inclined to read deep into the copy.

The problem with most current market research is that it tests in a manner that puts everyone in the third group—those inclined to read the whole copy, which, as biofeedback shows, most of us ignore.

When these long-copy ads are tested in focus groups, they inevitably end up having an unnaturally high chance of winning, especially because all that extra copy gives the study participants plenty of things to say during the questions. It helps them look smarter, too, because it allows them to rationalize aloud to themselves and to the interviewers why, yes, indeed, the superior product really *is* superior.

Figure 3.1 What appliance is more well known or easily understood than a refrigerator? This amount of copy can only be meant as assurance. Meant to sell to college administrators in a setting where information is sacred, it provides facts to argue from for what is really a no-brainer. (Reproduced with permission of the Mac-Gray Corporation. The MicroFridge® logo and MicroFridge® are registered trademarks of Mac-Gray Corporation.)

Because product managers are or at least try to be half in love with their products, they don't see a problem with long-winded copy. It's the proud parent routine of "Can I tell you all about how well my kid is doing in school?" Therefore, none of the testing reflects how things work in real life, as I will discuss in further detail in Chapter 4.

Ironically, the long copy does at times have a justifiable reason for existing, except that it's probably not the one the product managers had in mind in granting their approval to the ad. Here it is:

The long copy serves as a blanket that readers can wrap around themselves to justify a decision they've already made on an emotional basis. Just make sure you set up the story first. Give them a great visual and headline—that's 80 percent of the story for the first, second, and third group of readers alike (see Figure 3.1 for a good example).

Give consumers the story and give it to them fast, because without the initial sensory-emotive connection, there's no basis or need to reach for the rationalization.

Direct Mail: Heaven or Hell Scenarios

In direct mail, the great truism is that it's the list, the offer, and only then the creative execution. However, more often than not, marketers rely far too heavily on demographic and even psychographic profiles when creating a direct mail campaign. Unfortunately, these profiles run the risk of being insufficiently reliable, and the danger lies in missing deeper ways to connect with consumers.

As I discussed previously, our decision-making process is unconscious and emotionally driven by the leopard brain's amygdala. Therefore, the outer layer of cultural and social-economic factors isn't nearly as deep-seated as the psychological factors inherent to the species.

In other words, the oak-lined street along which the people live now won't ever be as important as the apple tree they remember from childhood.

Getting a better read on the target audience's inner voice lets a company decide who gets its message. But that's not all—it also lets the company plan when, where, and how the message gets delivered to hit the right emotional buttons.

> I'll pause now to look at the other big unavoidable truism with direct mail. It's widely accepted that there are three piles for how most people sort their mail:
>
> - Important
> - Kind of interesting
> - Trash
>
> To avoid getting your piece dumped into the third pile, don't shout your message.

The goal is of course to get through the clutter with an offer so compelling that it keeps on interrupting until action is taken. But shouting signals junk mail—and the trash can. It destroys any chance of securing an emotional connection.

If still alive past the initial sort, a package probably offers either the positive WIFM (what's in it for me?) of hope or the negative WIFM of fear.

It's a heaven or hell dynamic. Obviously, there are lots of qualifiers here, like the fact that if the hellish trick is too slimy it's sure to offend, or that in contrast to TV spots, with direct mail high-quality production can get you in trouble. Instead of conveying status and credibility, as is true on TV, slick is like shouting and can signal junk mail, too.

Strive for stickiness because recipients who hesitate are bait. By lingering with the mailer, they give you better odds at success.

Think of the long, winding road of hope that sweepstake entrants travel, in spite of being forced to follow complicated instructions. Their involvement is not a rational response—it's generated from the soul, not from the mind, and thus it's deeper and stronger. They see the complicated processes as akin to penance to qualify for the greater glory. The prospect of winning a sweepstakes creates an undeniable allure for many people that makes them want to go the extra mile. What can your direct mail piece offer that would be equally enticing?

Sales Brochures: A Very Short Story

Later in the book, I will discuss the concept of branding as story design. But for now, in relation to sales brochures, I would suggest that if there's any marketing medium where brand story design most literally applies, this is it. A company's literature—its brochures and other sales pieces—is like a very short story. It offers an introductory tale, told in print, to what a company hopes will be an attentive audience.

As I discuss in Chapter 6, there are many ways for increasing the potency and emotional resonance of your company's history. Remember these essential rules:

- To improve the odds of capturing interest, transform the story from nonfiction to fiction.

(continued)

- Move from too much copy that's too rationally oriented, to an emphasis on forging a sensory-emotive connection.

- Move your focus from your company as hero to the intended target audience as the actual hero.

- Above all, treat the literature as an initial opportunity to stake out your company's turf.

Again, I discuss these concepts in greater detail in later chapters. The lesson for now is that the trinity of your name, logo, and tagline is really just equivalent to planting your flag in the ground.

The truth is that there always seems to be another company out there that is cheaper or shinier, so planting the flag or serving up facts won't win the day. Instead, compete by building an emotional link, finding an edge, and being unique. If your company's visuals and words could be in a rival's piece, don't use them. Own a mental landscape that establishes yourself as invader, the protagonist of whatever offer category you occupy. Furthermore, reassure your potential customers that they will be winners if they align themselves with your company and your brand.

Sending out the literature isn't worth anything without a response mechanism. Most likely that means getting on the phone.

The strongest, most vivid emotional responses come from contact and interaction, so establish a dialog in which you get the opportunity to show—not tell— your story by using scene-by-scene construction that lets your audience see you leading them onward to success.

Catalogs and Circulars: Fend off Fear

By definition, most catalog readers want to say, "yes." Here's why:

- The odds are that through a previous purchase, or more proactively, by completing an order card, they chose to receive the catalog.

- Now they've opened it, and are looking through the pages.

- They're predisposed to make a purchase, and nothing is more vital to achieving a successful outcome than to keep the train on the tracks.

What can cause a derailment? The answer is fear. If clothing is involved, for example, there's the fear of the wrong size, wrong (higher) price, or wrong (cheap) fabric. The unknown is the great underlying fear because—in sensory terms—the offer must be bought on indirect sight alone. The transaction is entirely visual, because the reader lacks the reassuring advantage of using feel, touch, and smell to help tell whether the purchase makes sense.

What a smart catalog or circular does is to eliminate the readers' fear of being wrong or mistaken. Consumers naturally don't want to feel like they've been tricked. Anything outside the norm, including the legalese of disclaimers, creates an opportunity for fear.

Don't let the readers think too much. Don't let them get buyer's regret before they even complete the purchase. Con-

sideration stays active so long as our emotions, our judges of value, enable us to evaluate and frame the decision as free of harm and as something that just feels right.

Once a catalog has managed to keep its readers on track, the next goal is to make the journey as pleasant as possible. It's essential to keep the emotional connection intact because greater sales volume will follow from enhancing the initial connection in any way possible.

Keep in mind the three groups of print ad readers, because catalogs are really just a collection of print ads strung together. Plan for the in-depth readers. Make sure the copy can hold up. But mostly think about the following factors: Make your catalog clear, inviting, and easy. Create a visual-and-headline hook for the other, larger group of consumers.

With the movement from consideration to persuasion on a more unconscious level, the key is to convince readers that their rate of return for investing time in the catalog looks promising. Keep the emotional pay-off high and the sensory workload low.

Incorporating some "air" (white space) and a simple format improve the consumer's experience. A good-better-best format succeeds, too, but reverse the sequence so that the most superior product is presented first. Be sure to establish a psychological "yes" pattern rather than a "no, no, maybe."

From order form to phone call, every touch point should guard an emotional pay-off that involves the anticipation of receiving the order as much as its actual delivery.

Web Sites: Information on the Go

In spite of the dot-com bubble bursting, there's no doubt that Internet commerce is still a viable (and growing) medium.

The Internet is a medium still shaking itself out. It's new enough that suggesting what the rules are may not be as valuable as comparing it to media with which we've been working for years. Nevertheless, there are some ground rules I can offer.

- Like TV, the Internet is a highly visual medium. It requires dominant imagery to grab and guide consumers. Unlike passive TV viewing, in which time slows down, when we get involved with the Internet, we end up setting our own pace. We click onto the next page when we want to do so. Therefore, the Internet provides a sense of immediacy and interactivity that's not a major factor in other media.

- Like radio, the Internet is very intimate. We surf the Web in a private world that provides us with a feeling of discreet distance and security, comparable to the one-on-one quality of radio. The Internet shares this sense of security and actually expands on it by being able to turn a simulated conversation into a true dialog through interactive sites.

(continued)

> - Like print, the Internet has, of course, imagery, headlines, and text. As with print ads, long copy doesn't provide assurance and is often doomed to fail in this fast-paced medium.

As for direct mail, brochures, and catalogs, these media have their points of comparison with Web sites as well. But there are two other media I haven't covered yet that bear more relevance. One is outdoor advertising. Why? Because most of us zoom by the pages on a Web site, granting them about as much opportunity to grab our attention as we have time for with the typical billboard along the highway. Like outdoor ads, the Internet succeeds on just a visual and a handful of words.

Finally, even more crucial as a point of comparison in critiquing Web sites are retail environments. Or to be more specific, fast-food restaurants, which are the epitome of instant gratification and transparency. Think of McDonald's, with its simple floor plans and its menu board that we can absorb, complete with pictures of what we should expect our food to look like.

The truth is that most Web site designers could gain a lot of insight by hanging around McDonald's. The reason is that the McDonald's restaurant design is the definition of simplicity, with bright colors and predictable layout. We're a species that through evolution has learned to equate survival and comfort with being able to gain a quick, reliable sense of whether a given vista or situation presents promise or peril or if it's of no real, meaningful consequence.

In short, we want to be readily oriented.

If only Web sites could accomplish this feat more often. As it stands now, the world of the Internet is so cluttered that it makes Times Square look sparse by comparison. In addition, getting around within most Web sites isn't nearly as easy as it should be.

Adhering to McDonald's formula would behoove many Web sites. Designers should serve up the content hot and fast, wrapped like tiny presents. Like fast food, the content may not be especially nutritional, but little bites will do the trick so nobody chokes. The biggest enemy a Web site has is often itself: too much (empty) content.

The service for a Web site should facilitate grab and go and be friendly about it. Slow-to-load video and top-heavy pages lack immediacy and therefore alienate visitors. People won't wait or scroll down. As for access, in fast food land, location means being near interstate on/off ramps. On the Internet, let us get on and off the information highway quickly and without the distress of getting lost. Make sites clutter-free and easy to navigate.

Outdoor Advertising: TV's Twin

One way to think of outdoor advertising is to return to my 60/30/10 print ad rule and starve it half to death. By this I mean that the percentage of readers who would even have the time (much less the inclination) to read anything in depth shrinks to almost nothing. Unless they're driving and stuck in traffic, or on foot, the third group of conscientious readers simply disappears.

As for the middle group of readers willing to go a little bit beyond a quick glance, it verges on extinction, too. That leaves the first and, fortunately, largest group of "readers." The people outdoor advertising must aim for are those who can get their head turned, their curiosity piqued, by a single visual, a single idea, and in most cases preferably no more than five words of text.

I could go on to compare outdoor with direct mail because for both of them placement is essential. For the mailers, it's the list. For outdoor, it's location. But the more insightful link is to bypass print, direct mail, and even the literal or metaphorical car-culture mentality of radio and the Internet.

> TV advertising and billboards are like a pair of twins, separated at birth, very different and yet incredibly alike. Consider the following:
>
> * With TV, the medium is in motion. With outdoor advertising, the viewer is in motion.
>
> * Both TV and outdoor advertising are devoted to visuals. TV offers a short, 30-second drama as "movie." By comparison, outdoor advertising can be thought of as an even shorter, micro-second promotional trailer.
>
> * To create an effective billboard means putting into action the argument that, with any TV spot, it should be possible to reduce it to a single compelling visual and not need to read the text at all.
>
> * TV advertising rewards simplicity. Outdoor advertising demands it to hit sensory-emotive pay dirt.

The upshot of outdoor advertising's radical simplicity is that it's beneficial—if not downright necessary—to punch a conceptual ticket we're already carrying and have used before. Great outdoor advertising stresses clarity over cleverness, and it stays very close to imagery and situations with which we're already familiar.

Finally, both outdoor advertising and TV forge their connections with consumers primarily on a quick, unconscious basis. Remember that a good TV commercial references instead of trying to communicate an entirely new story. The same is even more true for outdoor advertising. Use a visual or a key word to trigger one of the basic, deep motivational issues that drive us as a species. For more about these innate drives, see Chapters 8 and 9.

Most of all, remember the following: Make sure it resonates, because with outdoor advertising, size makes anything dull only that much worse.

Store Environment: A Nice, Big Closet

A retail setting gives companies the kind of opportunity to connect with consumers that Walt Disney so eagerly seized in creating Disneyland. Remember, in the realm of his theme park, Walt was able to expand the sensory bandwidth beyond the sight-and-sound dimensions that were too limiting for him in print cartoons and cinema. He created a total sensory experience that is carefully rehearsed and expertly executed. This experience draws in consumers and makes them lifelong fans.

> The lessons that Disney learned in making films and then applied to Disneyland and Walt Disney World provide the template for what any store designer should address.[1] These include the following:
>
> *(continued)*

- *Visual literacy.* Disney wanted his park to provide clear sight lines for the guests so that they could easily "read" where they were going—and take the visual bait that would propel them along.

- *Visual violations.* This was Disney's pet peeve, his concern that attractions within the park must not displease the eye with something that might be either out of keeping with the other elements around it or something that was simply ugly.

- "Weenies." This was Disney's term for the sensory clues, both large or small, that rise to the level of becoming the great, compelling details that capture our attention and stay in our memory.

  The retail settings that master those three terms—engaging every sense and building a subtle yet clear-cut hierarchy of clues to guide consumers—are likely to be effective.

There are also other ways to engage consumers with the retail environment. For one, the emotional pay-off also needs to be in place. Consumers must not only be turned on, they must be tuned in as well, and that's where vivid sensory clues threaten to leave us if our attentive emotional response doesn't advance to the consideration stage.

In that second stage, emotions serve as judges of value. They tell us what feels right, and they reflect the goals and the frame of reference we bring to a situation because emotions are the product of personal meaning. They measure the odds of gain versus harm, comfort versus worry.

There, again, Walt Disney is pertinent because in the theme parks he knew to sell people what they already knew and could comfortably accept. He sold them Main Street U.S.A, small-town mid-America near the end of the nineteenth century. (Much of this came from his own childhood.) He sold consumers Cinderella's Castle, a fantasy drawn from fairy tales and the result of thorough research into European models. I could go on, because these familiar clues abound in the theme parks. The lesson here is for designing retail settings, and it goes as follows:

> *Think familiarity. In daily life, we tend to go where we've already been. As shoppers we seek a store that reinforces our inner vision of who we want to be, and that will give us the emotionally reassuring "strokes" that help make it happen.*

The store becomes, essentially, just a nice, big walk-in closet version of what we already have at home, either quite literally or at least in our own heads.

In-Store Displays: Guerrilla Warfare

As children, we learned the story of how the American Revolution began. The Americans along the road to Concord stood behind trees and shot at the British troops marching in tightly organized columns.

Now think about point-of-purchase (POP) displays. Frankly, they're a lot like the Americans in that war. Even at their very best,

Figure 3.2 Faced with challenges like lack of shelf space and easily damaged displays, POP creators have now cleverly resorted to floor graphics to catch our eye. (Reproduced with permission of Wetzel Brothers.)

POP campaigns are never as formal or as well equipped as TV commercials or the other leading forms of marketing. And yet POP can win the war for companies because it's right there along the front lines, where the action is.

After all, POP is usually within three feet of the point where consumers interface with a product on the shelf (see Figure 3.2). Such proximity is of vital importance because it's estimated that 70 percent of all purchase decisions are impulse buys that happen within the last five seconds before the decision is made.[2]

A good POP display is therefore in position to influence the proceedings and tip the balance in favor of one product over another. It involves the following factors.

- It works best by leveraging spontaneity.

- Sensory impressions hit us quickly and mostly unconsciously. Emotional responses typically form within three seconds of sensory exposure.

- Therefore, a display's five-second window of opportunity is perfect. It puts POP right in time with the dynamics of forming a sensory-emotive connection.

POP works on impulse, exactly the opposite of what the British troops were allowed to do. Furthermore, there's a second way in which the guerrilla warfare analogy holds up. That's because the British and American styles of fighting that war reflected a gap as large as the one between neoclassical (rational) economics and behavioral economics.

The former is straight-laced and supremely rational. It imagines us as fully conscious decision makers, taking orders from the learning brain as our headquarters. The behavioral economists are, on the other hand, accepting of the idea that people are intuitive and driven by emotions.

Smart POP doesn't get trapped in a neoclassical, utilitarian model that sees consumers as rational. It stands behind the tree and shoots, so to speak.

Instead of hawking selection, price, or other rational benefits, POP prompts a purchase on this shopping trip and another one the next time around by connecting on a deeper, fundamental level. In short, it fights on the home turf of emotion.

Packaging: This Baby's Mine

Packaging is truly first person. I pick it up. I carry it to the check-out counter. I open it at home. It's mine. Packaging is also intimate, and it involves a chance to promote commitment by inviting touch.

Why is touch so important?

- *Science has found that the very act of touching changes body chemistry.*
- *Touch prompts basic biological, sensory-emotive responses that show just how substantial the mind–body connection really is.*
- *For example, in developing his method for facial coding, researcher Paul Ekman was amazed to discover that the act of moving facial muscles to create an expression and simulate a particular emotion actually caused him to feel different and to take on that very feeling he only meant to imitate.*

Touch leads to reinforcement, and a company should aim to stop shoppers passing down an aisle. The goal is to get consumers to pause and to reach for a package based on a sensory-emotive connection that must be instantaneous and involuntary.

Grabbing the package should almost be like going for the baby that's otherwise going to fall off its chair. The internalized emotional connection has to happen almost that quickly, that unconsciously.

A company can bellyache about the uncontrollable factors standing in the way of making a strong connection, factors like the store lighting, shelf space, and placement. However, there are many design elements available to make packaging effective, such as the label, imagery, color scheme, shape, size, and texture. I believe there's one point related to packaging that companies are vastly underestimating, and that's weight. I'm talking about the actual size, the volume of the contents, as well as the number of ounces in the box.

The amount of air in the bag of snack food versus something you can actually eat is a good example. In terms of making a strategically important emotional connection with consumers, a company can't afford to create in us the sensation that we've been cheated, lied to, or tricked. That experience produces anger. It sacrifices long-term credibility for the short-term gain of being able to hold the price point while reducing the deliverable. Think of how a company feels whenever a supplier does that to it. Then think of how a consumer feels about such an outcome. Instead of life-long loyalty, the likely result is life-long defection and antagonism.

Consider L'Oréal and its bold, smart theme of "You're Worth It." We're all attracted to quality. We may not be able to afford it always. But we recognize it, respect it, aspire to it, and are eager to believe that we qualify as high-quality in some way ourselves.

You can just imagine the emotional distress if the content of L'Oréal's packaging—by volume or product quality—should ever be less than satisfactory. It would be like going from "You're Worth It" to "You're Worthless" instead. The package and product design is crucial for conveying the confidence-affirming message projected in the ads.

Product Design: Beyond Single Parenting

In real life, running a single-parent household can range from a choice to a necessity, and it can work well or not at all. But in business and in particular regarding product design and development, a company simply can't afford to rely on a talented industrial designer who acts as if the solo parenting of a commercial product is a viable option.

We've probably all heard the cliché about how anything that involves creativity—including products—runs the risk of being the creator's love child. To mention only risk without also mentioning joy is unfair because for the outcome to be successful, the act of invention must have engaged a product's creator so fully that he or she poured all of his or her passion into fashioning something great.

The problem is that if the focus ultimately rests on the creator, instead of the end user, then that's not the kind of offspring that consumers are likely to love. Companies are wise to avoid self-involved product creators because of the high risk that the creator has blind spots about any possible faults in the product. These are faults that consumers will clearly see and will have to live with if they buy and use the item.

What kind of risks am I talking about? One such risk is of course that it just doesn't work or doesn't work well. This happens especially when the creator becomes so enamored with certain aspects of the design that the basic issue of whether the product functions gets overlooked.

A second risk is, if anything, even more irritating—the product works, but consumers can't figure out *how* it works.

Ultimately, consumers long for clarity and ease of use. This longing speaks to a desire to regain a sense of control. The helplessness, stress, and discomfort we feel if we can't easily understand how a product operates will blunt—and may preclude—our ability to ever really deeply appreciate the product in the way that matters most: emotional pay-off.

But enough about possible faults, let's also look at the potential upside of a great product. The ideal solution for superior product design is combining the creator's passion with a commitment to others.

A great product truly brings consumers magic. Think of the Volkswagen Beetle or Apple's iMac, for example, and how their shape has become a brand element in its own right. Their design defines them—and it helps define and enhance our lives in much the same way that the original Coca-Cola bottle remains a treasured, familiar, reassuring presence that transcends basic commercial intent.

A great product works both functionally and on the sensory level because products are very physical and offer wonderful experiential possibilities.

But in the end, it's the emotional buzz we get through positive interaction with a product that wins us over. A great product has the following qualities:

- It provides a sense of freedom and connectivity with each use.

(continued)

- It reaches beyond the clichés about fitting our lifestyle because what's inside of us isn't a lifestyle—it's life itself. Almost magically, the creative spark that is in the product becomes something we also experience.

- In the end, a great product is easy. It makes a person say, "I like that."

- A great product becomes the winning example of what the competition should aspire to, and with that result, the winners get re-created—not in reality but in our emotional response to them.

Offer Design: Lie Low on High Ground

I sat through years of graduate school, and the phrase I remember above all is: "Control the discourse." What this means is that you win by imposing your perspective, your vocabulary, so that it then becomes the dominant way in which everyone frames a given issue.

I use this idea of controlling the discourse on behalf of my company every day, and it has profound applications to business in general. One area of particular importance is in offer design: in other words, how a company designs a product or a service or, even more likely, some combination of the two. At times, it even applies to something too intangible to buy, such as the Sturgis Rally for bikers that Harley-Davidson doesn't directly sponsor but tacitly endorses because conceptually Sturgis showcases the brand's outlaw, no-limits appeal.

With offer design, grabbing mental space becomes at once both the goal and the site of battle. A company is looking for space that at present is either badly defended, underutilized, abandoned, or has never before been explored.

Which of those descriptions fits doesn't matter. What does matter is that it's space worth taking, is in tune with the psychology of a company's sensory-emotive connection with consumers (or enhances it), and can be defended.

Take the initiative. Seize the high ground. That's how the original McDonald brothers got started before Ray Kroc entered the picture.

- First, they made a franchise based on a simple menu, low prices, and fast service. That was the start, but as with any offer design, there will always be a reaction by rivals.

- The next step is to lie low. Don't stand up and stroll around on the high ground because that's arrogance and will make it easier for a rival, sharp-shooting company to pick you off.

- As you lie low, plan the next step, the countermove. For a time, the McDonald brothers had female carhops deliver the food. They were sexy, and that was the problem. Teenage boys were the primary audience that was attracted by these women. *(continued)*

- The antithesis of domestic tranquility is teenage boys hanging out, marking their territory, and scaring off other men as well as women not looking to mate. Their aggressive sexual presence may not have actually disrupted service, but it posed a real danger to the heart of the offer design.

- The McDonald brothers' new move was to focus on being an all-American family entity, a safe place to bring children. The atmosphere and every aspect of the experience had to reassure parents and soothingly align with their strongest protective urges. The McDonald brothers got rid of the women carhops because business really is like war, and in the end the only allies worth having are customers.[3]

The McDonald's success is obvious, and they in effect owned the category of fast food that they created. They tailored their offer exactly for the audience they wanted to attract; in doing so, they initiated a franchise that few could rival.

Customer Service: Up Close and Real

Nothing is more emotional and dangerous for companies on a daily basis than customer service, and it can feel like a no-win situation. Good customer service is an expectation, taken for granted; on the other hand, bad customer service is a sin that is rarely (if ever) forgiven. A company will of course be tempted to rationalize and to disregard the problem because, well, you know, people can be such a pain.

Bad service is death for a company. Not dramatically, but more like a thousand small knife cuts.

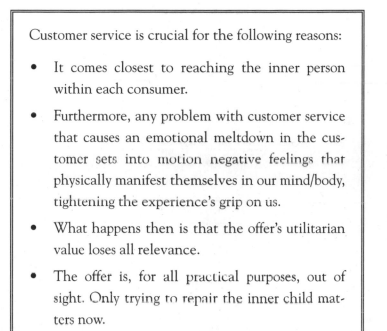

Customer service is crucial for the following reasons:

- It comes closest to reaching the inner person within each consumer.

- Furthermore, any problem with customer service that causes an emotional meltdown in the customer sets into motion negative feelings that physically manifest themselves in our mind/body, tightening the experience's grip on us.

- What happens then is that the offer's utilitarian value loses all relevance.

- The offer is, for all practical purposes, out of sight. Only trying to repair the inner child matters now.

Good luck—extracting the poison will take time. First, the staff will need to practice empathy, as opposed to inducing more stress. They will need to give the customer a chance to feel like there are resources available, resources that can be brought under control to restore security. Finally, after rebuilding a sense of security, the consumer will gradually find comfort if not a renewed opportunity for pleasure.

The lesson is that customer services meltdowns cost a company its hard-won emotional brand equity—not to mention the hard, emotional labor that staff must put in to repair a damaged relationship. Therefore, the strategic investment of avoiding such scenarios is well worth it.

Walt Disney didn't leave customer service to chance, and neither should other companies. Basic, tactical-level analysis is a part of a proactive solution. A company should fully map out the customer service experience, choreographing each and every step of the story to build in value and anticipate problems.

On a deeper level, a company should also analyze the emotional framework of the customer service experience. They should determine what the customer's expectations and needs are and seek new ways to meet them.

This degree of analysis might seem like overkill, but it offers a far better strategic approach than waiting to be killed slowly by inferior customer service. Tolerating bad customer service creates the risk of undermining and even defeating successful efforts involving all of the various consumer contact points that have been covered earlier.

Now that I've discussed marketing strategies in different media, I turn to marketing research methods that truly tap into how consumers feel about products, offers, and campaigns.

Notes

1. Kathy Merlock Jackson, *Walt Disney* (Westport, CT: Greenwood, 1993).

2. Joe Rabaglia, "A Strategic Approach to Developing Effective In-Store Programs," speech presented at the P-O-P Show, New York, September 4, 2002.

3. Eric Schlosser, *Fast Food Nation* (New York: HarperCollins, 2002), 19–21.

The New Research

Understanding How Consumers Really View Your Products

The stumbling block every marketing research department inevitably faces isn't even about getting good data. Their first problem is simply getting funded by the CEO.

Of course, the CEO wants to know the answer to the following: "Why shouldn't I just buy some more advertising placement rather than spend money on a report nobody will read?" Asked that question, I answer: Part of the reason Confederate General Robert E. Lee lost at Gettysburg is that his cavalry scouts got lost in the Pennsylvania countryside. Lee simply didn't know what he was facing.

> *Good research reduces risk and helps deploy resources more effectively. You can't get ahead of your rivals without getting closer to consumers, and good research helps you get there.*

Nevertheless, given the reliability and usefulness of most current marketing research, I'm not sure I wouldn't opt for the extra advertising myself at times. Research is worthwhile primarily to the extent that it captures what people actually do or how their bodies react in real time.

Data based on verbal input, filtered on a conscious basis, doesn't guarantee accuracy—no matter how many people are interviewed.

What about the researchers who resist the new scientific findings, new insights about how the brain works, and the implications of all this for the business world? They scare me because researchers are paid to be smart, inquisitive, open-minded, and searching for answers.

Most of all, these skeptics remind me that there were once also a lot of people invested in the idea that the world was flat. But when Christopher Columbus sailed the ocean blue, as we all know, he didn't fall off the end of the earth.

Researchers are paid to be, in effect, the accountants of marketing, to make sure everything creative is panning out. For the open-minded researchers, the curious, those looking to do their job better—and for the marketing types bored and dubious about the status quo—this section of the book stands ready to offer new criteria and tools to match what science says.

The Challenges to Current Marketing Research

Cognitive science, behavioral economics, experiential marketing, evolutionary psychology. As we head ever farther away from the millennium, and into the twenty-first century, the forces of change seem to be everywhere. Everywhere, that is, except within the field of marketing research.

There are exceptions, of course. At a conference held near the turn of the millennium, speaker Christyne Dzwierzynski of Unilever described the research industry as "ripe for a revolution." Soon another speaker, Doss Struse of Knowledge Networks, agreed, saying of the field that it "remains based on 1950s' mass marketing and 1940s' service models."[1]

Just as the earlier eras of branding persist, the research that supports brand marketing is, despite innovations, frequently a holdover of the rational, utilitarian mindset of the neoclassical economists and the late great Adam Smith. This paradigm is grounded in the idea of the consumer as rational and was predicated on features-attributes-benefits campaigns. A new model is needed to capture the dynamics of the consumer decision-making process as science has now revealed them.

Based on the new scientific model, there are four criteria any marketing research tool must be able to address to remain viable:

- *Conscious versus unconscious*. Given the estimate that the vast majority of our mental activity doesn't occur on a fully conscious basis, any methodology that can't access more intuitive reactions isn't robust enough. In fact, it's almost not worth doing; who would pay a land surveyor only to count the treetops?

- *Real time versus mediated*. Because emotional responses often occur within three seconds or sooner, slower, more consciously derived responses are likely to be both inadequate and insufficiently reliable. Good data only comes from

(continued)

---

real-time testing. This timing is especially crucial in a world where consumers are deluged with marketing and advertising messages; they make immediate decisions about which messages to listen to and which to ignore.

- *Sensory-emotive versus rational.* The high-and-low-roads model of consumer decision making shows that the amygdala, our brain's emotional thermometer, plays a major role in how we form assessments and make our decisions. Any tool that ignores or underestimates feelings has to be reconsidered because humans are largely emotional "thinkers." Meanwhile, failure to take into account the initiating role of sensory impressions is another equally large blind spot that research must address.

- *Verbal versus nonverbal.* Most experts agree that 80 percent or more of communication is nonverbal, so why settle for accessing the little information that's available aloud? Verbal comments are likely to be less emotionally open, are susceptible to spin, and are more prone to issues of interpretation. In general, verbal statements are unstable in trying to handle the demands of crossing international or cultural barriers. Marketing research must move in the direction of testing for nonverbal reactions and responses to products and offers.

The Ability to Get below the Surface

Let's see how well the existing marketing research tools fare when pitted against the criteria listed. I'll start with the top two investigative requirements: the ability to access unconscious reactions and to do so in real time.

With the unconscious, the stakes are extremely high. Not only is conscious thought merely the tip of the iceberg in terms of mental activity, but our real decision-making process—prior to rational confirmation—happens in a matter of split seconds.

In other words, to learn how consumers are responding is like trying to hit a moving target. It's not easy, but the rewards are phenomenal. Clearly, monitoring customers in real time is worlds away from the traditional, sit-down focus group interview sessions. Such focus group sessions are freeze-framed events. Subjects sit in their chairs and answer questions. Among its shortcomings, the focus group format must fight against years of classroom memories and ingrained etiquette, as well as typical group dynamics, which turn most of us into self-conscious rather than unconscious "thinkers."

In contrast, by sticking close to what people actually do in given situations, such as when marketers follow a consumer through a real store, observation can capture the more unconsciously driven behavior. In terms of what people do (as opposed to why they do it), observation is in fairly good shape as a research tool vis-à-vis the new scientific criteria for what constitutes good research.

Even more intriguing in terms of their potential ability to access reactions that lie below the surface of awareness are tools like hypnosis and projective techniques like photo sorts or image-gathering. What consumers might say while "under the spell" is incredibly interesting. Meanwhile, the kind of photographs or imagery that people either choose from a preselected deck of options or gather themselves through the materials that matter to them in their lives is certainly laden with unconscious influences.

On the downside, hypnosis does best capturing what wells up inside of us; therefore, anything new—a product or an advertising approach—may not elicit much response. As to image gathering (less so for sorting), there's the issue of whether the data is being collected in real time. However, the chance to see how people perceive the world is valuable. After all, the basis by which every research tool must be judged is the sense-feel-(think)-do model.

> Hypnosis is oriented to internal "vision." But our selection of imagery relates to the first stage of external, sensory impressions. Remember the cliché that a picture is worth a thousand words. My company uses a trio of geometric forms as an alternative test mode for the companies that aren't ready to try biofeedback because it gets us to the concrete, the specific, in real time and with the opportunity for unconscious influences to come into play.
>
> There are still the issues of how to quantify the data and what they mean. We have normative biofeedback readings already in place for each geometric form. We also chose forms that we had explored in previous independent research to determine their appeal across cultures.

Finally, there are several other traditional tools that I haven't covered; the primary examples are data modeling and surveys. Both methods are problematic when the criteria involve accessing the unconscious in real time. They're too abstract, too removed from the initial sensory stage of our decision-making process to reveal the unconscious workings of the brain and thus to yield real insights into how consumers feel.

Good data modeling works from what a person did or bought or selected as a feature. But the context—the sensory clues—are missing, and the analyst working with demographic variables can't overcome that absence.

The same holds for most surveys conducted by phone or, at times, at a mall—again, these settings are missing the clues that help drive decision making. In that respect, surveys that are conducted over the Internet, with the stimuli shown, have a slight edge over traditional surveys. However, the question of whether the responses are occurring in real-time becomes the issue instead.

The Ability to Get a Sensory-Emotive Reading

Because we are all primarily emotional decision makers, the second vital ability that any good research tool should have is the capacity to quantify gut reactions.

How could it be otherwise? After all, what the senses absorb and the body feels profoundly impact the mental processing to follow. To achieve more marketplace penetration, companies must therefore gain a richer, more intimate understanding of consumers in a business context that inevitably focuses on the human body.

Nevertheless, in the age-old debate between seeing consumers as driven by reason versus passion, most of the conventional research tools are more at home with reason. They're ill equipped for the task of reliably gauging whether a sensory-emotive link exists between a company and its target audience.

The major exception in orientation—though not in its deliverables—is focus group research. Well suited to brainstorming exercises, focus groups are meant to get the participants all revved up. Sometimes they work—even if only the lead dog really gets going. But when it comes time to assess the input, the energy level and tone of voice with which a comment was made are too easily discarded.

I've met with researchers for some major advertising agencies. I've heard that in their sessions they always make sure the videotape is of good enough quality to enable review, but I've never gotten much of a sense that they systematically quantify in any way the body language of the people involved in the sessions. I've also never observed that the reports are indexed to reflect nonverbal clues that might indicate whether the comments are whole-heartedly meant or are merely throwaway lines that people use to paper over silence.

> Now let's look at the alternative research methods. They include the following:
> - *Observation of consumer behavior* tracks peoples' bodies, such as when they move through a store aisle. The subjects can also be outfitted with eye-tracking devices that register where they look, what part of the print ad gets noticed, and which stack of boxes or cans generates more apparent interest.

> *Otherwise, none of the common research methods address*
> *physical reactions.*

As for emotional responses, I challenge you to name one technique that doesn't ask the participants to think their feelings. In the case of secondary research, emotions aren't even a factor.

Here's a rundown on why traditional marketing methods are flawed:

- *Regression analysis* uses variables like volume of sales relative to price point; clearly, this misses the mark on the four criteria I laid out in the beginning of the chapter.

- With *surveys*, you're getting attitudes, not feelings.

- *Laddering* can be a useful technique for identifying deeper levels of meaning, but it's still a cerebral exercise.

- The same can be said for *word associations* and *sentence or metaphor completions*. They're like playing Scrabble.

- As for *storytelling* or *cartoon drawings*, those are, indeed, emotionally oriented, but they pose other problems—like how best to interpret the results and whether the method itself is actionable and repeatable. Furthermore, because the emphasis

(continued)

> with the cartoons is really on the captions inside the balloons above the characters' heads, then both the drawings and the stories are actually verbal mediums of research—which, as I'm now going to address, is another can of worms entirely.

The Ability to Go beyond Verbal Input

The third and final measure of what any good research tool needs to be capable of is reaching beyond the comments of study participants to discover something more complete.

Why harp on the suspect quality of verbatim transcripts? There are two excellent reasons, the first of which is scientific in nature. No talk in this book of how the species is "hard-wired" through evolution is thorough unless it addresses the role that language does and doesn't play for us as consumers. The reality is that our ability to communicate verbally came later in the evolution of the species, with the learning brain.[2] Therefore, words can't always readily capture what the more sensory-emotive leopard brain perceives and feels.

Even on an individual basis, think of how we come to understand the world. First, we react to physical signals. In time we begin to communicate orally; only later does the written word play a role. So is it any wonder, then, that the accepted statistic among linguists is that at least four-fifths of how we all communicate is nonverbal—a percentage not unlike the degree to which unconscious thought predominates.

Here's an even more in-depth critique: In *The Silent Language*, Edward T. Hall concludes that of the 10 primary modes humans use to communicate, only part of one of those modes involves actual verbal language. The other nine modes are nonverbal. Moreover, the role of purely verbal communication may be even smaller than one-tenth because verbal communication is routinely influenced by nonverbal signals we deem to be more credible (see Figure 4.1).[3]

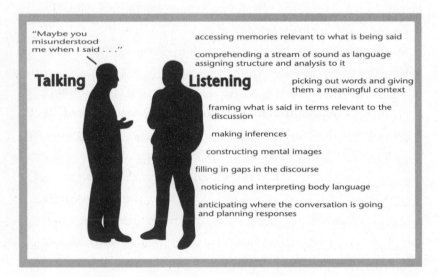

Figure 4.1 Verbal communication involves a rich interplay of factors that greatly complicate the ability of researchers to direct questions, gather responses, and understand consumer responses. (Illustration created by Maria Williams from ideas presented in: Hall, Edward T., *The Silent Language* [New York: Anchor Press, 1981].)

Furthermore, studies indicate that a conscious-level verbal test method has about one-in-ten odds of being truly accurate.[4]

You can begin to see why verbatim messages are inadequate. (I haven't even gone back to my point in the introduction that, of course, people also commonly neglect to tell each other the "truth" because we spin, deflect, hint, or hold back all the time.)

The second reason to harp on the quality of verbatim messages is that in spite of their dubious nature, marketing research casually and unquestioningly relies on them a lot. In a company's direct mail campaign, it would kill for an extra 3 percent increase in response rate; a low-end number is never acceptable. Why, then, do companies overlook their failure to capture the other, missing 80 percent (or more) of how we communicate?

Focus groups are totally verbal, as is laddering (sequential probing). Surveys are totally verbal, if you count the written word. Techniques like observation or eye-tracking rely on gauging emotional reactions through verbal responses. Even worse are word association, storytelling, and sentence or metaphor completions.

What does that leave? Among more conventional research approaches, there are two kinds of options available for anybody wanting to go beyond verbal input. One is photo sorts, drawings, or imagery gathering. For this the medium is nonverbal, but the line of interpretation often reverts to soliciting verbal, conscious-level responses. Finally, the other options are data-driven approaches like secondary research and choice modeling, which don't involve words because direct, living, breathing consumer input is entirely missing.

Getting Closer: Psychophysiological Research

This book's title, *Body of Truth*, arises from observation by scientists, psychologists, and myself that the human body won't lie. To put it more precisely, our bodies embody and reveal our reactions whether we know it or not.

Mind/body veracity doesn't mean we can't manipulate our physical reactions. We can, but not nearly as well as we may think. Nor does it imply that we don't engage in trying to hide or obscure our body language.

> *Contrary to speech, physical reactions are much more difficult to hide, due to the largely unconscious and spontaneous nature of emotional responses to stimuli.*

The bottom line is that by observing our automatic reactions, science can read the body pretty well. After conducting the preliminary research that went into founding my company, I concluded that my best bet for helping other companies get closer to consumers was to get closer physically. I decided to return to the basics, and nothing is more basic than the human body—including how it reflects our initial sensory-emotive reaction to marketing efforts and shapes our purchase behavior to follow.

> *Psychophysiological testing is a live, "blood, sweat, and tears" sort of evaluation.*

One irony of marketing research is that the word now most commonly used to judge a consumer's more conscious, rational response—our *attitude*—is rooted in body language instead. During the eighteenth century, the term *attitude* was typically used to talk about art. More specifically, *attitude* then meant the posture or pose of statues or people in a painting. This old definition resurfaces any time a telemarketer calls to ask about our position or stand on buying a ski vacation for two.

Today, what marketing research needs to do is redirect the term—not to its eighteenth-century artistic roots, but as Darwin used it, to mean the physical expression of an emotion. A renewed emphasis on the human body is important to marketing research because only then can it reliably gauge gut reactions. Presently, about the only way that the physical body enters into research—other than during taste tests—is as a distracting element during focus groups when to look around at the other participants is likely to be far more interesting than the session itself.

The solution to marketing research's current shortcomings is credible mind/body research. This research provides measures to verify both the clutter-busting impact and the loyalty-inducing appeal of a branded offer. Some of these tools use overt, observable means, whereas others employ technology to monitor what the eye can't see but the body feels.

The best of these mind/body research tools offer a fair degree of objective measuring; therefore, the scores can be used as norms for the purpose of creating a repeatable methodology.

Sensory-Emotive Research Requirements

The special requirements involved in focusing on sensory-emotive analysis pose a real challenge to current marketing research. Part of the challenge is to reevaluate traditional tools in light of the new scientific criteria that I outlined earlier. But another, even larger part goes beyond any specific tools. The issue is recognizing and fully accepting the conceptual shift necessitated by the new sense-feel-(think)-do model of decision making. In short, researchers must adopt an entirely new mindset to focus on consumers' sensory and emotional bandwidths.

Let's consider the sensory realm first. To gauge its effectiveness, Walt Disney was said to have gotten down on his knees in his theme park at least once to learn what a six-year-old child would see. It's hard to imagine most CEOs doing the same thing, but surely gaining a better handle on how consumers perceive a company and its offer is necessary. It's hard to assess consumers' perceptions of your company or product in an effective, unbiased manner.

Walt was brilliant and went with his instincts. For the rest of us, the trick is to find a reliable research tool up to the task. Once we find the right tool, the strategic advantage is immense. The best way to beat your competition is to gain a better understanding of your customers, not in the abstract but in the extremely specific ways they choose to purchase from you rather than a competitor.

The simple truth is that the sensory realm has to be tested in a sensory manner. Here's why:

- *Sensory input is quick, and intuitive.* Now it's time for a trick question. Where does the hippocampus, our sensory filter, operate? You could say in the leopard brain, and you'd be right. You could also say below the radar screen of conscious awareness, and you'd be equally correct. For com-

(continued)

panies, the mind/body concept signals that access to what is in consumers' heads requires an understanding of what is happening inside their bodies on a spontaneous, real-time basis.

- *Sensory input is rooted in specifics.* Researchers must avoid a fundamental mismatch between their content (sensory clues) and their mode of inquiry.

  Clichés exist for a reason. Sayings like "seeing is believing" and "follow your nose" acknowledge the value of not straying too far from actual, physical, concrete perceptions. To put it another way, what Walt was really doing by getting down on his knees was to simulate the "magic camera" inside all of us. He realized the strategic business value of trying to watch the movie we film inside our heads. In that way, he could hope to gain some, at least secondhand, sense of the mental imagery—rooted in perceptual sensations—that makes up the magic camera film footage always playing on our not-so-big internal screen. We go there to watch our thoughts, memories, projections and fantasies.

- *Sensory input is beyond articulation.* Our senses take in much more information than we can consciously process. But there are other factors, too; one is, again, a large mismatch between content and the medium of inquiry. Because we think in images, not words, research pursued on verbal grounds alone is like a fish out of water.

The other big factor in why sensory input is beyond articulation is that words are very limited in what they can capture and express. Our reactions may be colored by vague factors, such as a smell or a color association, but we can't consciously identify these factors as the root cause of our reactions. Indeed, the body's perceptual abilities vastly outstrip the ability to articulate those kinds of subtleties. Human understanding of the world flows from bodily experience, which a scale for verbal ratings can't even begin to quantify.

As to the emotional realm, many researchers have already come to respect its power and significance, but in many cases, they have been stymied because they lack the means to delve into this new area of research. In addition, one could argue that it's far easier to ignore the need to test emotional reactions by instead immersing yourself in recording conscious, rationally oriented attitudes.

Here's why the switch to emotions must happen:

- *Emotional responses differ from rationalizations.* Again, the decision-making process runs, in effect, from sensory impressions to attaching emotional significance to those impressions. Then and only then do we get around to conscious, rational, attitudinal responses. What goes on rationally is a lot like confirmation. We rationally form a justification to a conclusion that we have already arrived at on a sensory-emotive basis. For a researcher, accepting ra-

(continued)

tionalizations is to be tricked by what is often polite surface chatter.

Think about how often in our daily lives we establish a need for the rational—and then make an irrational choice instead because it's what we really want to do. There will always be stock market bubbles because we still willfully believe in what we suspect is unrealistic.

- *Emotional responses come from deep within.* Given the large role that the unconscious plays, it is not surprising that consumers inherently possess a limited grasp of what motivates them. A rational approach to research is akin to thinking of consumers as a machine that you can open up and tweak a bit to work better. In that view, changing a few of the offer's attributes is as simple as changing the oil in your car. In reality, discovering what motivates consumers is not so easy, nor is it so rational and mechanistic. To gain a richer understanding of consumers and their responses to an offer or a company's positioning of it, good researchers must come back to the look and feel of what's under scrutiny. In other words, they should walk along the leopard brain's neural back alley to the amygdala and see if any hot buttons got pressed (see Figure 4.2). I'll discuss methods for accomplishing this shortly.

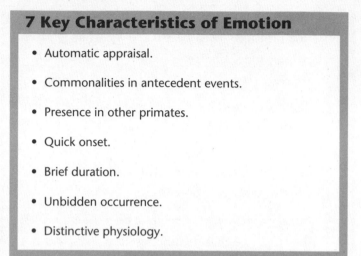

Figure 4.2 Seven Key Characteristics of Emotion. (From material presented in: Ekman, Paul, and Richard J. Davidson, eds. *The Nature of Emotion: Fundamental Questions* [New York: Oxford University Press, 1997].)

How to Measure the Sensory-Emotive Realm

Accessing the sensory and emotional realms is challenging, but the rewards are considerable. As in everything, there are strategies, tools, and techniques. In a moment, I will address the two non-branding research tools at which I arrived in my search for a means of exploring consumers' sensory-emotive reactions; in addition, I will provide insights into how they work.

First I want to step back a little and discuss how the sensory-emotive realm should be measured. The reason for this is because however a company chooses to approach this vital realm, it will need to know the means by which to gauge success. Of course, the temptation is to continue to rely on verbal self-report data, with binary (yes or no) data or ranked data (on a numerical scale). However, these scoring systems are as flat and unidimensional as the world was once considered to be.

Scientific studies indicate that the correlation between how we interpret our emotions and the kind of physical response that we actually have runs no higher than 10–15 percent accuracy.

In short, we're nearly blind about what's going on inside ourselves.[5] The body is the key to reading consumers, and the way scientists and psychologists, with a deeper understanding of the human body and psyche, measure our responses is always a matter of impact and appeal.

The benefit to businesses of using tools to read the body is that it enables them to find out what consumers are actually feeling intuitively. With this information, companies can then establish the kind of instant likability that can drive preference and loyalty.

Mind/body research ensures that your offer has both impact and appeal.

By only securing impact, your offer is like a ship whose sails are full of wind but with no rudder. It's racing along, but nobody can tell if the ship is headed toward or away from shore, toward or away from landing consumers' approval. In contrast, appeal without impact means they would have been won over—if only they had noticed your offer.

Perhaps you're asking yourself which of the two variables is more decisive—impact or appeal? The answer is inevitably that it depends on the marketing objective, the medium of application, and even sometimes the kind of target audience involved. What any market researcher is looking for—and gets paid to do—is to assess consumer preferences and motivations. A combination of impact and appeal provides the crosshairs on the sight for doing so.

Research must involve context as well as content, and with an impact-and-appeal compass, a researcher can be more on target in selecting the winners from the also-rans and in diagnosing likely improvements in the marketing efforts.

The Mind/Body Research Options

In practical terms, the new mind/body concept means that companies looking to get inside our heads must first understand what is happening inside our bodies. It can't be otherwise because, as a species, we're holistic. All systems are intertwined. We're bodies, hearts, and minds—and every part has to be taken into account to form the equation.

To do so, there are many psychophysiological research options to help gauge the visceral, gut reaction. Given the criteria cited earlier in this chapter, some tools emerge as obviously more robust than others.

The easiest group of tools to start with involves the overt, body language options. Although these are the ones visible to the eye or otherwise fairly detectable, the exact meaning of the results they provide is an issue at times.

Help gauge gut reactions with these body language clues:

- The subset of *body posture and movement*, *hand gestures*, and *proxemics*, which refers to the study of physical proximity. These methods are rela-

    (continued)

tively easy to monitor—at least in broad terms—and perhaps almost as easy to classify, but they're also susceptible to distorting factors, such as self-conscious posing, body image, gender differences, and cultural display rules. Therefore, their meaning is hard to judge.

- A second, visually oriented subset consists of *gaze (or eye-tracking) and pupil dilation*. These tools are not as easy to monitor as broad body language. They also assume a link between attentive gazing or pupil size increase, on one hand, and consumer impact or interest level on the other. Perhaps even more problematic is that, except by verbal means, they are ill equipped to measure appeal.

- Finally, two other overt options include *vocal analysis*, a promising method that is still the subject of much academic debate, and *facial coding*—soon to be covered in greater detail.

The second group of options requires direct, sensor monitoring to record changes in bodily systems. Most of these measures offer the advantage of being very precise and immediate, but they also involve touch.

These options include the following:

- One subset consists of such doctor office tools as *checking our heart rate, blood pressure, pulse, respiration,* and *temperature*. Like eye-tracking, they can gauge impact but can't quantify appeal.

(continued)

> • A second subset of brain wave type tools include
> the *electroencephalogram (EEG)*, and *CAT, MRI,*
> *and PET scans*. These tools are intriguing but ex-
> pensive, not easy to execute, and even harder to
> interpret.
>
> A less invasive technique than these and one
> with more of a substantial track record is *biofeedback*,
> next on the agenda.

Biofeedback as Sensory Research Tool

Of all the mind/body research tools introduced in the previous section, biofeedback best suits the special requirements involved in
gauging consumers' sensory reactions to brand marketing stimuli. Its
single greatest strength is its ability to be distinctively sensitive to
quick, transitory reactions.

Biofeedback offers a good means of capturing sensory re-
sponse data in real time and on a spontaneous, unconscious
level. Moreover, it's very objective and precise, it provides
highly actionable data, and it can address both the impact and
the appeal of whatever branded offer concept, product, or
marketing execution is being tested. The bonus is that biofeed-
back isn't speculative.

Indeed, biofeedback has been in use for decades, and many of
the kinks have been eliminated. One aspect of the technique dates
back to the mid-nineteenth century. By 1925, biofeedback in general was already on its way to becoming a heavily documented re-

search tool, thanks in part to Carl Jung's use of it in word association experiments.

What exactly *is* biofeedback? It's a blend of psychology, biology, and electronics (see Figure 4.3). Its most common use is as a treatment method in which a psychologist will monitor a person's biorhythms to help change his or her functional behavior. Thus, biofeedback is often employed to improve patients' ability to cope with stress. Among its many practitioners are the Mayo Clinic and the majority of the country's other leading medical research institutions, as well as NASA, which has found it helpful in training astronauts.

When applied to business, biofeedback is perhaps more appropriately thought of as biosensing because it's being used not to change but to measure sensory responses. It does so using the body's own natural electricity.

Our sympathetic nervous system is based on a group of nerve cells that communicate by sending high-speed electric signals to each other. Biofeedback involves the use of tiny sensors to "hear" the original electrical message of the cells as they communicate. This tool allows researchers to access—in real time—the true sensory reactions of consumers before those reactions are translated and reorganized by the rational, learning brain.

The importance of such access is that there is, as the saying goes, no second chance to make a first impression. In scientific terms, biofeedback measures which sensory impressions get taken in and fed to the amygdala, our emotional thermometer, thereby setting the decision-making process in motion.

Biofeedback is, accordingly, a means by which companies can assess initial reactions to a host of stimuli. For instance in what we call stationary testing, my company uses biofeedback to test partici-

Biofeedback

Q **How does it work?** Impact is measured in terms of skin conductance level (SCL) by placing sensors on the fingers to record the degree to which a stimulus arouses interest. That level is gauged through the electrical correlate of sweat gland activity because sweat contains salts that make it electrically conductive. SCL increases in a linear relations to the number of activated sweat glands and is measured by the amount of electrical current that the skin will allow to pass in units known as mhos (ohm spelled backward, and defined as the reciprocal of resistance).

Appeal is gauged via electromyography (EMG) by attaching small, noninvasive electrodes onto the face. These skin readings track how much a person likes or dislikes a stimulus by measuring the electrical correlate of smile (zygomatic) and frown (corrugator) facial muscle contractions. EMG measures the electrical energy given off by the nerves that signal a muscle to contract, with the appropriate electrical unit being the microvolt (one-millionth of a volt).

Q **How is biofeedback different from a lie detector test?** The polygraph test does not detect lies, but rather signs of emotion. Wires from the polygraph are attached to the suspect to measure changes in sweat, respiration, and blood pressure. Increases in blood pressure or sweating are not in themselves signs of deceit. Hands will get clammy and the heart will beat faster when any emotion is aroused. Polyography leaves the realm of science when it assumes that basic arousal processes occur only when someone is lying. Lying and excitement, from a physiological standpoint, look identical.

Figure 4.3 Biofeedback. (From materials presented in: Schwartz, Mark Stephen, *Biofeedback: A Practitioner's Guide*. [New York: Guilford Press, 1987].)

Figure 4.3 (*Continued*)

pants' reactions to TV spots, print ads, direct mail, circulars, and other promotional items.

Being the son of an interior designer, I was inclined to go to real-life situations and test people's reactions in spaces like store environments, restaurants, or, most dramatically, inside various car models. For this, we have mobile biofeedback; it gives us real-time, real-life biofeedback readings that capture responses on the go.

Facial Coding as Emotive Research Tool

We engage in conscious, rational thinking largely to validate the sensory-emotive-based decision we've already made. In short, our three-part brain follows the heart. As consumers, we choose between offers on a primarily emotional basis. We listen to our feelings. And we listen to others, whether it seems like we do or not. The interaction that leads to empathy means that often our emotions come from the anticipated, imagined, or recalled outcome of face-to-face social encounters.

Darwin also realized that humans are social creatures whose faces reveal and communicate emotions, whether we know it or not. The adaptive advantages to being emotional thinkers abound—for example, emotions help us focus. They speed our actions, and they also help us communicate and learn from other people's signals. All of these factors contribute to making facial coding a robust research tool.

The French anatomist Guillaume Duchenne originally aided the scientific study of recognizing emotions through facial muscle movements. In 1862 he published photographs that showed the results of using electricity to stimulate face muscles. A decade later Darwin published *The Expression of Emotions in Animals and Man* based on correspondence with Duchenne and using his photographs and others taken for the purpose of comparing laughter and crying. Darwin argued that emotional reactions were ingrained in the human species and that emotions are universal.

For nearly a century, the development of facial coding went unfinished. One reason was that the social scientists and neoclassical economists who dominated the thinking of this era endorsed a model according to which cultural (not mind/body) factors supposedly carried more weight in shaping motivation than does being hard-wired as a species.

Facial coding's leading practitioner, Paul Ekman, picked up the trail again.[6] In addition, legendary facial coder Silvan Tompkins and the emergence of new research have helped challenge and invert the old motivational model. Our inner mind/body state is now regarded as a far greater influence than external, cultural factors. Indeed, in studies conducted around the world, including among New Guinea tribes who had seldom been exposed to other people, Ekman found evidence to support Darwin's belief in an evolutionary continuity that links expressions and mental life. The practical result is that Ekman and other facial coders have developed systems to interpret facial muscle activity. Now companies can truly read how consumers are emotionally responding to brand positioning, offer design, and marketing executions among other applications (see Figure 4.4).

There are, of course, some limitations to these methods, including issues of gender. Women tend to be more expressive than men in the studies we've conducted. However, the muscle activity evident on women's faces doesn't look any different. In accordance with Ekman's system, the same basic seven emotions are still evident. The extent to which activity takes place varies; as long as the sampled population matches the target audience, the issue of expressive versus nonexpressive respondents is moot. In addition, with facial coding it's possible to read how emotions mingle or replace one another.

As for other factors, age is not an issue for the same reasons just given. Darwin got his start with facial coding by looking at his own children's expressions; at my company, we have tested people as young as six years old or approaching eighty.

As for ethnicity and race, again, part of what makes facial coding so powerful is that it sticks with just those core emotions that transcend boundaries and unite us as a species. Like biofeedback, facial coding is tremendously useful in marketing because it goes deep and wide, testing among universal reactions.

In short, facial coding reliably crosses ethnic, racial, as well as cultural lines, providing the kind of research tool companies have always wanted and will especially need in the new, internationally integrated economy.

A Profile of Facial Coding

• **Background** Beginning in the 1960s, Paul Ekman (University of California, San Francisco) and Wallace V. Friesen began to systematically study the physiological correlates of emotion. Their work took them around the globe and, after seven years of intensive analysis, they developed the Facial Action Coding System, or FACS, now in use in psychiatry, by the law enforcement community (FBI and CIA), and also by computer animators at Pixar (*Toy Story*) and DreamWorks (*Shrek*). Although there are other coding systems, FACS is widely regarded as the single most comprehensive method available. It's the gold standard in the field.

• **Method** FACS is based on the facial muscle movements that accompany facial expression because consistent patterns have been found in expressions across cultures. An *action unit* (AU) is defined as the minimum, visible, anatomically based action involved in the movement of the face. There are 43 identified AUs located across the face's three regions: (1) brow and forehead, (2) eyes, eyelids, bridge of nose, and (3) cheeks, nose, mouth, chin, and jaw. A facial expression is described in terms of the particular action unit that singly or in combination with other units produces facial movement. FACS shows which of these AUs constitute the expression of seven basic emotions: sadness, anger, happiness, fear, surprise, disgust, and contempt. False versus genuine smiles can also be detected because they use different muscles.

• **Scoring** Study participants are videotaped either during one-on-one interviews or while viewing or experiencing the stimulus being tested. A second-by-second analysis of the videotape is then conducted to reveal the AU's that can be reliably distinguished when a facial movement is inspected repeatedly in stopped and slowed motion. Full expressions last only a few seconds on average. There are also "micro-expressions," with involuntary muscle movement "leakage" that will often reveal in a fraction of a second what the subject is actually feeling.

Figure 4.4 A Profile of Facial Coding. (From materials presented in: Gladwell, Malcolm, "The Naked Face: Can you Read People's Thoughts Just by Looking at Them?" *New Yorker* [August 5, 2002].)

Summary Critique of Research Methods

In accordance with both the traditional requirements for marketing research, but especially the new criteria as indicated by the break-throughs in brain science, here's an overview of the relative merits of each approach:

Traditional Analysis Methods	Psychophysiological Methods
Focus Groups • Good for brainstorming, immediate surface-level emotional and verbal input, and sensing what's socially acceptable. • Exploratory, descriptive, offers the opportunity for showing stimuli, to establish rapport and probe. • Major weakness is bias of both group dynamics and moderator's influence. • Risk of securing what is expected, acceptable, "fits the agenda." Low likelihood of accessing feelings or unconscious reactions. Gain only mediated, filtered, public responses.	*Biofeedback* • Chance to gain direct, unfiltered access to transitory emotional states and unconscious reactions. • Precise, objective, real-time readings of otherwise subtle, even invisible reactions. • Use of sensors will create some degree of self-consciousness and physical inhibition.
Surveys • Opportunity to gauge attitudes, gain statistics for simple analysis. • Except by Internet, usually conducted in abstract, so no sensory stimuli. Because it gains input retrospectively, it risks the fallacies of memory. • Chance to misrepresent feelings or failure to gain access to them. Low commitment level by participants. • Problem of leading questions and ambiguous phrasing. Solicits general response, not specifics, or emotions.	*Facial Coding* • Gains real-time access to emotional response, so you can learn the motivational potency of stimuli. • Accesses both conscious and unconscious reactions, often through brief, micro-expressions involuntarily revealed. • Need to draw participant pool correctly to allow for gender differences (men are less expressive). Best to phrase the questions so that they invite spontaneous reactions. *(continued)*

Figure 4.5 Summary Critique of Research Methods

Summary Critique of Research Methods

Traditional Analysis Methods	Psychophysiological Methods
Choice Modeling • Rigorous diagnostic exercises to pinpoint and isolate influential variables. Rigorous data-sorting. • Uses past behavior to predict future behavior. • Data may not be sufficient, accurate, up to date, or relevant. • No ability to access nonverbal, unconscious responses. Research is conducted in the abstract, without sensory clues. • Interrelations of independent variables could make it unreliable to interpret.	*Eye Tracking* • Opportunity to gauge with some real-time precision what catches the eye, how quickly, and how long the subjects focus on it. • Can't access appeal except through verbal solicitation of reactions.
Observation • What people do is more reliable than what they say. Behavior will involve both conscious and unconscious impulses. • Conducted in real time, with loads of sensory data. Follows the narrative of what people do. • Involves translation or self-interpretation of data. • In interviews, it risks leading questions and ambiguous phrasing. What does the behavior mean? Hard time knowing "why" people do what they do.	*Vocal Analysis* • Helps sense energy level apparent in response. Considerable evidence that emotion produces change in respiration, phonation, and articulation. • Gets at intangibles, available tonally. • Ability to read emotions with accuracy is possibly limited to sadness and anger. • Need to separate impact of elocution and diction from signal read-out transcript.

Figure 4.5 (*Continued*)

In very few professional fields could the state-of-the-art be so far behind the times, scientifically speaking. Marketing research must catch up to where neurobiology has led, and here are a few of the criteria by which to measure progress (see Figure 4.5 for a summary of new methods). Therefore, I conclude this chapter with another top 10 list.

Top 10 Rules for Marketing Research

1. Access the Unconscious

Nothing more directly challenges status quo market-ing research than the emerging scientific consensus that almost all mental activity isn't fully conscious. For market research, this revelation means that as study participants we have only a limited knowledge of our own responses and motives. In short, we don't really know what's going on. This realization under-mines everybody's sense of self-control. It also casts profound doubt on the completeness, reliability, and thus the actual validity of any research techniques that take for granted a totally or even largely con-scious reasoning process. How can we possibly self-report reactions or purchase intentions when we can't really know what they are?

In seeking to access and reveal the unconscious roots of consumers' thought processes, there's a need to capture the actual, real-time perceptual imagery and memory-based imagery inside us, as well as the net effect of this stimulation and how it impacts our evaluation of a company's offer.

Three goals are the most important in tapping into the unconscious:

- *Gauging consumers' intuitive reactions;*

(continued)

- *Measuring those reactions reliably;*
- *Understanding what they mean.*

Although the third goal is hard even for psychophysiological tools to access, the use of rotating test variables offers a way to investigate hypotheses on a nonverbal basis.

2. Focus on Nonverbal Output

Verbal input alone is too shaky for companies to rely on.

The reasons why can be broken down into three broad categories. The first involves communication problems created by having an agenda. Companies ask questions that reflect an agenda and inevitably bias the outcome. Participants sense the agenda, and they're inclined to answer positively to the question to be cooperative, take the path of least resistance, or avoid appearing ignorant.

The second reason that relying on verbal input alone makes for bad research is that it doesn't fit the new scientific insight that most thought is unconscious and rooted in specific sensory imagery. In contrast, verbal input is consciously mediated and, most often, vague and abstract in nature. Third, words are hard to use, interpret, and quantify. This is a problem likely to get worse in today's increasingly mass-media,

(continued)

postliterate society, as clear articulation is becoming less and less important.

3. Gauge Emotional Responses

Perhaps nothing better illustrates the split between gauging rational versus emotional responses than the research snafu involving New and Classic Coca-Cola. The data came back supporting New Coke, predicting its success on the rational, utilitarian grounds that it tasted better. But the data failed to capture the depth of consumers' emotional connection to the old product.[7]

The new scientific insights about the high and low roads along which we form sensory-emotive and then rational responses to the world around us clarifies Coca-Cola's error.

The low road of an emotional response happens first, and it predominates our decision-making process. In contrast, facts are malleable. We can move facts around until they align with our gut reaction.

The important lesson for other companies is to avoid repeating Coca-Cola's mistake by seeking and granting importance to emotional responses. In addition, we must recognize that neither the old pen-and-paper or verbal input approaches can accomplish the vital task of gauging emotional responses with any

(continued)

great accuracy. The reason is because of the mighty role of the unconscious and what we can't or won't say.

4. Never Forget the Sensory Clues

To be effective in the marketplace, you must become a sharp detective and discern which of the sensory clues truly connect with consumers and which fail to perform up to expectations. Sensory perceptions play a central, initiating role in the decision-making process. Their relative ability to trigger the right emotional response is crucial. Food companies conduct taste tests and perfume companies laboriously investigate scents, but it's amazing how few other companies honor the senses in their market research. The physical world is, after all, the one in which the offer exists. The same is true of the other touch points that support the offer in seeking to nurture our urge to purchase it.

> To leave alone the sensory bandwidth is to move into a realm of abstractions, where few if any of us exist very often or for very long.

Surveys and choice modeling rarely if ever dip into the sensory realm. Observational techniques come loaded with sensory clues, but the problem is determining which clues are relevant to the offer being marketed. Finally, in focus group sessions the

(continued)

most interesting stimuli are inevitably not the moderator's questions but the other people in the room.

5. Gather Data in Real Time

Instant replays happen on TV but not in real life. Consumers live in the moment. We make our decisions within a few seconds, often less. In other words, we form an impression and act on it. Consumers are like the players on the field, whereas most marketing researchers are like the referees. The unfortunate thing with this set-up is that the guys in the striped shirts aren't the ones who score and make the game exciting. They have rulebooks and seek to impose rational order, whereas consumers have instincts and rush for the end zone.

Consumers live in real time, so a company trying to capture reliable data must do likewise. Sensory clues that survive our intuitive filtering and hit an emotional hot button speak the language of action, not reflection.

Our assessments of what is interesting and pertinent happen instantaneously, on a largely unconscious basis, so research that allows for greater, prolonged conscious deliberation misses the heart of the matter.

(continued)

6. Enable Intimacy

To provide valuable, useful insights, marketing re-search information has to be gathered in a manner that enables it to have some depth. Otherwise, it's the old garbage-in, garbage-out syndrome. To gather only superficial input is like the end of *Casablanca*, when the police are told to "round up the usual suspects."

Superficial data may complete the project assignment, but it won't help a company identify and act on opportunities to create a stronger sensory-emotive connection with consumers.

To accomplish that vital goal, a company must instead conduct its research in a way that can make participants feel both comfortable and significant. More likely than not, the way to do so is through a one-on-one interview. We want a face across the table so we can judge for ourselves whether the interviewer is someone with whom we're willing to open up and trust, even a little. Getting in touch is the cliché that suggests the personal connection that should exist, even if briefly; without it, consumers won't internalize the questions and reveal where they find the emotional pay-off in a company's offer. Without that connection, it's far easier to retreat to

(continued)

defensible, rational answers—answers that ultimately distort reality and aren't sufficient to explain why consumers favor one branded offer over another.

7. Ensure Validity

What company wants data it can't trust enough to justify its decision? To avoid this scenario, a company should achieve both internal and external validity for its research by taking these three steps:

- Adhere to a test procedure that is as free of bias as possible;

- Use psychophysiological methods to gain solid data;

- Engage in objective analysis.

The reason researchers should go the mind/body route is because the body has a much easier time being on target (than does verbal input) given the large role of the unconscious in making real-time reactions. Moreover, by using scales of measurement that adhere to the body's biological systems, a natural, less arbitrary system of analysis gets enacted. The benefit is a smaller sample size than is possible with conventional studies.

(continued)

There's greater precision in measuring specific, physical reactions tied to emotions than there is in relying on verbal, surface responses.

8. Establish Reliability

To clarify the relationship between the validity and reliability, the analogy of shooting at a bull's eye works. Validity of the data corresponds to accuracy— that is, being able to hit the inner ring, the bull's eye. That concept is easy to grasp. As for reliability, in this analogy it's the same as consistency, or getting the shots to fall close together on the target. When a company gets tightly grouped shots that land within the bull's eye and the diameter and placement of the bull's eye doesn't vary, then it has achieved both validity and reliability—the ideal result.

How does this analogy apply to current market research and how it needs to improve? Right now, reliability is easier than validity for most marketing research techniques to achieve. Large sample sizes and recurring test methods that have been carefully honed over the years may enable the shots to be practically on top of one another, but who knows if those shots are really in the bull's eye or in the outer ring of the target?

(continued)

When there are correlations to actual, in-market performance (people's purchase behavior), we can accept the results.

9. Provide Crisp, Actionable Data

Senior management needs to have the following things:

- Data it can trust that are valid and reliable;

- Data it can understand that are crisp and accessible;

- Data it can act on; in other words, data worth funding because strategies can be built around them.

For the results to be of use when emotions are being investigated, marketers need to pay more attention to the key variables of impact and appeal; most marketing research has overlooked these items.

Scientists understand that impact and appeal are key measurement scales. Look at almost any scientific study that gauges people's responses or evaluations of concepts and stimuli, and you'll find that one scale is essentially impact. To scientists, this is the same as potency or arousal. In business, this means the ability to break through the clutter and arrest and hold the attention of consumers.

(continued)

The other scale that many scientific studies use might be called appeal. To scientists, it's called valence or evaluation. In business, this represents the sense of likability that can drive preference and loyalty.

Impact without appeal makes judging almost any marketing outcome impossible.

Right now, too much of the marketing research captures surface chatter. It doesn't tap into the deeper, sensory-emotive dimension in which consumers make decisions and determine a company's market share.

10. Understand the Context

It's crucial to gather good data in a manner that fits the new scientific, sense-feel-(think)-do model, but additional study is needed to explore why certain sensory clues survive conscious and unconscious screening. Attention and selection is after all only the first stage of the perceptual process.

Three stages are integral to both the hippocampus's selection of clues and the emotional significance that the amygdala will attach to them. They are:

- Organization;

- Interpretation;

- Retrieval.

(continued)

> All three stages rely on how people categorize clues, seeking similar perceived features to then form a model that allows for less conscious processing. Because these models help shape perceptions and are difficult to change once established, marketing research must investigate them. Exercises like regression analysis, which estimates the relationship between variables, represents a start. But its rational, utilitarian mindset and, in particular, its assumption that an independent variable creates change in the dependent variable is far too simplistic. In comparison, science indicates that our network of mental models, stored as memories, is more like a maze of branches, infinitely harder to measure.

Now that we've looked at how research must change to measure the way consumers actually react to stimuli and make decisions, the next chapter turns to using emotive branding to make irresistible offers.

Notes

1. Christyne Dzwierzynski and Doss Struse, quoted in *Research Conference Report* (January 2001): 1.

2. Terrence W. Deacon, *The Symbolic Species: The Co-Evolution of Language and the Brain* (New York: Norton, 1997), 28–39.

3. Edward T. Hall, *The Silent Language* (New York: Anchor Press, 1981), 196.

4. Margaret M. Bradley and Peter J. Lang, "Measuring Emotion: Behavior, Feeling, and Physiology," in *Cognitive Neuroscience of Emotion*, ed.

Richard D. Lane, Lynn Nadel, and Geoffrey Ahern (New York: Oxford University Press, 2000), 244.

5. Ibid.

6. Macolm Gladwell, "The Naked Face: Can You Read People's Thoughts Just by Looking at Them?" *New Yorker,* August 5, 2002: 38–49.

7. David B. Wolfe, "What Your Customers Can't Say," *American Demographics* (February 1998): 24.

Using Emotive Branding

How to Tap into Consumers' Deepest Emotions

L et's admit it straight away. In both theory and practice, the exercise of branding companies or specific offers can sometimes risk being incredibly, even ridiculously nebulous.

A common experience is that any time a discussion about branding, occurs "the quota of B.S." goes up dramatically. No one knows what anybody else is really saying. Suddenly, the air grows thick with every buzzword known to MBAs.

Nor can I say that my own introduction to branding years ago, when I began my career in business, challenges this experience. Still, branding can be valid, even essential, and it's here to stay.

> In this chapter, I'll address some crucial issues about branding:
>
> • How to improve it;

- How to curb the waste that often comes with developing a strategy;

- How to make it more substantial;

- As part of the process's viability, how to generate more buy-in from others within the company, starting with the CEO.

Right now, the lives of most brand directors aren't very easy or particularly secure. They often have to hope that nobody within the company has ever read (or remembers) the classic fairy tale of the emperor's new clothes. In a company, none of the employees dare admit to the CEO that the new clothes (marketing strategy) the tailor made don't really exist. He is standing in front of his subjects stark naked.[1]

CEOs don't like to be embarrassed any more than anyone else. You can see why it's rumored that the average brand director's tenure at a major company hovers somewhere around two years. Pedaling air has a short shelf life.

To get to something real, anybody responsible for branding in any way would be wise to orient branding around things more permanent. In fact, a good place to start is with what I've covered so far—the dominant role of the unconscious and the new sense-feel-(think)-do model of consumer decision making. The bedrock to work from is that we are hard-wired through evolution to respond to certain basic patterns of existence.

In this part of the book, my focus is on bringing the power of the sensory-emotive connection into the discipline of branding. My primary goal is to establish a stronger customer-brand relationship by reaching back in time to what instinctively engages people. Throughout the span of human history, there are many patterns that suggest commonalities among cultures, and one of the most powerful, unifying phenomenon is storytelling. As I'll argue, the art of storytelling is something a brand must master to engage and win customers.

Get Back to the Basics

Before we get to the power of storytelling, let's look at the reason behind why it's so necessary today.

Consider the historical frameworks set up in a pair of valuable business books: James H. Gilmore and B. Joseph Pine's *The Experience Economy* and Rolf Jensen's *The Dream Society*.[2] These authors argue for the evolution of the species, not in scientific terms but in regard to ever more sophisticated social-economic models.

> To splice the two books together is to arrive at a quick march through history—in economic terms—that looks something like this:
>
> - *Getting by.* From an economic point of view, the earliest stage of humanity includes both the nomadic hunter-gatherer era and agrarian societies. What the wanderers and the settled farmers had in common was that they dealt with core commodities. They took what they could from the natural world—wild game, grains they could grow, metals they found in the earth.
>
> - *Getting going.* The second stage of economic development was the industrial society. This stage saw the dawn of factories and machines. This era began
>
> *(continued)*

in England around 1750. A century later, the United States was charging ahead. The time had come for basic goods—staples of existence like flour, beds, and soap—to be standardized. The dawn of manufacturing eventually led to new staples like cars, phones, washing machines, and so on.

- *Getting rich.* The third stage of economic development has been the information society. In the 1950s in America, the number of service jobs overtook the number of manufacturing jobs. A decade later, there were more people working at desks than on factory floors. At least in the developed world, this shift was marked by affluence. We could start to have customized work done for us the way we wanted it. Machines were no longer as important as knowledge or what people could carry inside their heads—planning, flowcharts, numbers, and so on.

The problem with the information society is that too much information becomes stressful and disorienting. People begin to block out messages perceived to be invasive or unwanted.

Indeed, consumers today face the following:

- *Going hungry.* Here we are today, strangely dissatisfied as consumers. We have it all, and more—scores of TV channels to view at home and everything we could want in stores. But now we want what we used to have as a society before everything got too complicated. We want to be physically moved and emotionally engaged. We

(continued)

long for what will be memorable and meaningful, something other than just another purchase. Pine and Gilmore call it the experience economy; Jensen has dubbed the new emerging era the dream society. Our response is to dismiss marketing that speaks to rigid, rational logic and touts product attributes. What we want is the chance to feel something, anything, other than stress (see Figure 5.1).

Society:	Agrarian	Industrial	Information	Dream
Offer	Core Commodities	Basic Goods	Essential Services	Optimal Services
Brand Phase	(Prebranding)	Traditional	Identity	Experiential
Orientation		Product	Mass Consumerism	Customization
Connection		Attributes	Imagery	Story Line

Figure 5.1 As the socioeconomic model has evolved, branding has made corresponding advancements. Another advance will be required of companies as we move deeper into the new "dream" era, in which the rational loses its appeal in favor of feelings and fantasy. (From materials presented in: Pine, Joseph. B., and James H. Gilmore, *The Experience Economy: Work Is Theater & Every Business a Stage* [Boston: Harvard Business School Press, 1999], p. 6. Jensen, Rolf, *The Dream Society: How the Coming Shift From Information to Imagination Will Transform Your Business* [New York: McGraw-Hill, 1999], pp. 6–19.)

The current psychological state of consumers has profound effects on branding. From the dawn of humanity to today's postinformation age (beyond facts to feelings), the authors find a progression that has led to consumers' sensory and emotional satisfaction being the key to future business survival and success. They argue that businesses must become people-centered and go back to the way we used to rely on our senses and feelings to navigate the world in ancient times.

We have made things much too complicated for ourselves and for consumers. We must now reduce stress by getting simple again.

Introduce sophisticated simplicity. Go forward by returning to basics.

The pressures of a saturated marketplace are too mighty not to seek competitive advantage anywhere you can. You have to stay close to consumers, and consumers in today's new dream society want optimal experiences.

Consider, for example, this observation from Sharon Lee of the Hollywood marketing firm Look-Look: "For young people now *it's pure raw emotion*—it's anything that inspires you to think 'I want that . . . because it fits me so well.' It can be a person, a product, a place, anything" (emphasis added).[3]

Companies take note: To stay relevant, branding must return to the first stage of existence. We're not talking animal, vegetable, mineral; we're talking (emotive) hearts and (sensory) bones.

The Previous Eras of Branding

In tandem with social-economic development, a similar historical movement has also been under way in regard to branding. The essential goals of branding have never truly changed—they include serving as a barrier to competition, avoiding commoditization, and being known in a world where face-to-face encounters are becoming less of the norm.

What has changed is branding's focus and its means of execution. Only the Romans (artisans engraving their names on items like sandals) and the Elizabethan English (liquor distillers marking their barrels) did any branding prior to the industrial age. Therefore, there have been three social-economic stages prior to now but only two branding eras.

The first, *traditional era* of branding began in the industrial age and persists even today. Its focus is on factory-made, mass-produced products. Its means of execution involves logos and taglines distinguishing otherwise anonymous goods. Although driven by fear that the products involved are indistinguishable commodities, this form of branding remains largely content to establish its name on products.

The second, *identity era* of branding came of age in the 1960s, when affluence was rising and the role of TV-inspired mass consumerism was growing. This era also lives on, and its focus is on the use of mass-media advertising to project an image, an identity, and at times a corporate voice. This approach had in its favor the power of emotionally oriented company imagery (sensory clues). Furthermore, the idea of creating a voice is effective because a voice implies somebody speaking—a person or at least something other than another anonymous corporate entity.

But, the second era of branding has always had the problem of relying on impersonal broadcasting. In today's fractured media arena, the problem hasn't gotten any better. Moreover, in the attempt to create a unified corporate voice most often heard through the mass media, a pair of questions weren't answered in depth. The first is, who's talking (what is the company's personality)? The second question is, of course, are the consumers truly listening (or is it a monologue)?

In short, this attempt through branding at establishing a voice has always been more internally focused than externally focused. It favored corporate consistency over making a connection with consumers.

The New Era of Experiential Branding

The new, third experiential era of branding seeks to create more intimate, unique experiences across the full spectrum of customer contact points. It recognizes that even identity branding leaves consumers with an overly broad and still fairly abstract mental picture of a company. It also recognizes as the bottom line that without reinforcement, any attempt to broadcast an identity doesn't adequately deliver. Such an approach simply doesn't get companies close enough to consumers to change the outcome in a highly competitive marketplace.

One reason why experiential branding can help is that it's more focused on the customer. Remember the traditional drivers of branding, such as creating a barrier to being a commodity and distinguishing yourself from rivals. These are legitimate goals, but they are also advantages enjoyed by the company, after all, and not for the benefit of its customers.

In contrast, experiential branding adheres to the reality that you can never forget the WIFM (what's in it for me?). Consumers inevitably focus on their own needs and rarely adopt a long-term view.

The first and second eras of branding—with the product as hero and the company as hero—won't work. Either approach means the customer isn't the hero.

Experiential branding relies less on rational product attributes than customer needs and strives to create a sensory-emotive experience for the customer rather than just broadcast an identity. Furthermore, experiential brand marketing isn't just customer-focused, it's downright intimate.

How do you get closer to your customers? As I've discussed, the answer is to get physical. Consumers' largely emotional decision-making process is triggered by their intuitive interpretation of sensory perceptions. Therefore, the concept of branding needs to be redefined. The brand as guarantee or promise of performance shouldn't be viewed as primarily a functional issue. Instead, consumers seek sensory-emotive assurance in a brand. We want to trust that it will provide satisfactory sensory stimulation as well as emotional comfort and pleasure. Thus, the new era requires not just a more holistic body, heart, and mind approach. It also means that companies must prepare for a far greater amount of brand-managed connectivity with consumers.

Think of experiential branding as a game of high-stakes poker. It involves greater, more strategically oriented contact with the customer, but at the same time, it also forces companies to nurture every touch point. What I mean is that the sensory clues or signals a company sends consumers during the brand identity and product promotion stages are significant, and they help shape the target audience's anticipatory perceptions. In addition, the sale and use stages are, if anything, even more important because we tend to experience our strongest emotions during contact and interaction with people (service) and objects (products).

The failure to make contact with consumers will jeopardize the sale. The failure of the product to live up to the branding promise is likely to result in no repeat sales and customer defection because of unrealized expectations.

The Importance of the Brand Story

Experiential branding is based on realizing that a brand is, for the consumer, really a series of experiences or take-away impressions. Together, they form the "story" of the brand-customer relationship (see Figure 5.2).

What is meant by brand story *can be defined in part by saying what it isn't: It's not the history of a company's origins and growth, although those details can contribute to the story; nor is it the straight narrative sequence of a single sales transaction, although again aspects of such an experience can play a role. A brand story is like a collage of sensory clues that translate into a coherent emotional pattern. This collage gets built over time based on the full range of the advertising, sale, and consumption of an offer.*

If there's any company that most effectively understands the importance of the brand story and, simultaneously, of the children's market, it's McDonald's. The menu-board items are only a small part of its story. The story elements of McDonald's include the setting and the playgrounds that are often found on the site. Other elements include the characters, most notably Ronald McDonald. In addition, there's a wide variety of imagery, symbols, and associations—ranging from the signature colors of yellow and red to the golden arches and toys that serve as promotional tie-ins (see Figure 5.3).

How effective is McDonald's? On average, 90 percent of American children between the ages of three and nine will visit McDonald's every month.[4]

Is Your Brand a Story Worth Remembering?

The issues that compel a company to reconsider its brand story status can come from any of three sources: (1) internal company-driven opportunities and needs; (2) external, marketplace dynamics; and (3) external consumer-driven perceptions.

Story Status	Branding Issues
Obsolete	Relaunching, repositioning Outdated image Changing customers
Weak	Low loyalty, loss of share Worried investors
None	Undifferentiated Underdeveloped or invisible image New markets
Confusing	Changing corporate structure Inconsistent image
Inadequate	New products, services, extensions Negative image New competitors

Advertising Age's Top Ten Icons of the 20th Century

Icon	Offer
1. Marlboro Man	Marlboro cigarettes
2. Ronald McDonald	McDonald's restaurants
3. The Green Giant	Green Giant vegetables
4. Betty Crocker	Betty Crocker food products
5. The Energizer Bunny	Eveready Energizer batteries
6. The Pillsbury Doughboy	Assorted Pillsbury foods
7. Aunt Jemima	Aunt Jemima pancakes, syrup
8. The Michelin Man	Michelin tires
9. Tony the Tiger	Kellogg's Frosted Flakes
10. Elsie	Borden dairy products

Figure 5.2 Is Your Brand a Story Worth Remembering? (Top 10 Icons reprinted with permission from www.AdAge.com. Copyright Crain Communications, Inc., 2003.)

Figure 5.3 For kids, McDonald's is a playground, a Happy Meal, and a new toy that is often tied to the latest movie attraction. (McDonald's™ and Happy Meal™ are used with permission from McDonald's Corporation.)

Ray Kroc has, in effect, one-upped his former World War I Red Cross unit colleague, Walt Disney, by offering Happy Meals that compete with the Happiest Place on Earth. A vacation to Disneyland or Walt Disney World might not fit in a family's budget, but a trip to McDonald's is normally financially and logistically achievable. Kroc made sure you never had to look too far down the street to find one.

As with Disney's theme parks, McDonald's child-focused strategy carries at its heart a brand story with lots of chapters. The emotional "strokes" that come with the bright colors, the toys, the playground, the Hamburglar, McDonald's-land, McKids clothing, and the rest are also a set-up for later in life. All of these elements represent a radical new form of brand equity.

Together these touch points create a story that taps into the target audience while it's still young—forging a sensory-emotive link that has the potential to be stronger because there are fewer if any competing brand stories in place to challenge it.

By tapping in early, the brand story has a longer shelf life. It offers the greater value of cycling through adulthood and being passed on to the next generation.

Meanwhile, even on a daily strategic basis, the brand story adds plenty of value for the company. What the golden arches and the rest of the story elements do for McDonald's is to give it a band-width for hooking customers that vastly exceeds the power of the food itself.

Consumer needs that may not be resolved on an immediate product level can still be redeemed on a deeper, more sustainable brand association level. In other words, the French fries may be cold, but a child's feelings for Ronald McDonald remain nice and warm, providing the branded experience with a protective layer to absorb disappointment.

The Storytelling Power of Mark Twain

By employing a Disney set designer and Disney songwriters to help build its brand story, McDonald's long ago aimed to appeal to the kid in all of us.

Stories and childhood form a powerful combination (see Figure 5.4).

Figure 5.4 People love stories. So is it any wonder that "Human memory is story-based. . . . We are more persuasive when we tell stories." (Roger Shank, *Tell Me a Story: A New Look at Real and Artificial Memory* [New York: Charles Scribner's Sons, 1990], p. 4.)

That's a fact well known not only by Ray Kroc but also by one of our country's foremost writers: Mark Twain. Drawing on his childhood memories of life along the Mississippi River, Twain created such characters as Huck Finn, Tom Sawyer, and Becky Thatcher. He also created a mental image of an era and setting that has been proven to transcend time by seizing the imagination of young and old readers alike. As much of an artist and self-promoter as Walt Disney was, Twain always paid homage to the role of the intuitive. "Authors rarely write books," he confessed. "They conceive them, but the books write themselves."[5]

A great believer in what today is called the unconscious, Twain respected and profited from drawing on the deeper, nonrational power of stories. He understood, as Disney did, that storytelling is powerful because stories offer the three C's that matter most to business in designing an offer and selling it: they're how people *conceptualize*, *communicate*, and are most readily won over or *convinced*.

For example, most jokes have a plot or at least a narrative logic to them. The way we seek the support of a loved one in telling about a problem at work is to talk it through from the start, building the story scene by scene. It isn't by chance that in Hollywood they ask, "What's the story?"

The truth is that human beings crave stories. As parents know, a child who sits enthralled through a fairy tale that imparts a moral is the very same kid who wouldn't bother to listen to—or grasp internally—that same moral had it been told straight out.

We are emotionally invested in stories, practically unable to pull ourselves away from a good one. In fact, science has confirmed that stories work the way the mind–body works. The leopard brain's hippocampus, the sensory filter, grabs lively details that get quickly passed along to the amygdala so that it can gauge their emotional temperature.

In the end, all of the value of creating an effective brand story gets delivered emotionally. Although the utilitarian level helps consumers rationalize their decisions, it will only get companies so far. Reason alone simply lacks enough of a hook.

In contrast, a great story captures and holds our imagination and draws us in. Yes, it gives us information. But it does so in accessible, emotional terms.

How does most information hit us these days? We don't trust it. We can't fathom it. So on a largely emotional level, we conclude that we don't or won't have enough time to deal with it.

Stories are different. They're (supposedly) fiction. They result from the willing suspension of disbelief, so in effect consumers don't even care if a company's brand story is true (in relation to the utilitarian, features-driven facts surrounding products). On the contrary, the product alone has to appear to be nonfiction. Even then we're not likely to know the facts behind it, care, take the time to learn them, or even be able to do so.

Instead, we care deeply about—and get a feeling for—whether the story is true to itself. Does it possess emotional integrity? Is it believable?

> *A brand story needs to resonate inside consumers. If we don't believe, we're offended by its failure to resonate.*

Fortunately, there are tricks of the trade to improve the odds of success and avoid inadvertently giving offense. In that regard, Twain can help companies craft their stories. In spirited, mock seriousness, Twain's essay, "Fenimore Cooper's Literary Offences," damns an early nineteenth-century American novelist.[6] But it also inadvertently offers rules for companies seeking to build brand stories that will work well. Twain claims there are 19 rules for good fiction or maybe 22. Cooper is said to violate 18 of them.

In essence, the rules fall into five categories:

- *Relevancy.* The elements of any company's brand story should be there for a reason. They

(continued)

should help the story achieve its goals and arrive somewhere. Extraneous sensory clues cloud the sensory-emotive connection and leave the story up in the air.

- *Clarity.* The story should avoid confusion and lazy effort—in other words, finding the right word beats using its second cousin.

- *Plausibility.* The company's projected personality as expressed through its voice should sound like a real person talking instead of grandstanding. The story should remain anchored firmly in the realm of the possible, unless a miracle is reasonably well presented.

- *Consistency.* Suspending disbelief requires a corporate advertising and design style that doesn't go both high-brow and low-brow at the same time.

- *Vivacity.* No story is worth anything if it bores you to death, or if its humor is implausible. Create a story capable of truly engaging an audience.

Finally, the most important rule is that the character of the company should be so clearly defined that consumers are reassured—knowing how the company would behave in case of an emergency.

Think of Johnson & Johnson's thorough handling of the Tylenol scare during the 1982 Tylenol murders in Chicago, in which bottles of the common medicine were laced with cyanide and seven people died. The company moved immediately to remove any potentially harmful products from the shelf and innovated the tamper-proof bottle design to prevent future scares. Consumers don't like surprises, and they want to believe that companies like Johnson & Johnson will live up to their brand promises.

Branding as Story Design

In effect, what Twain did in deliciously dissecting Cooper's inadequacies as a writer is to make the point that the tale must be protected from the teller. Anything that disrupts, dislodges, or—worse yet—prevents a sensory-emotive connection from getting formed is disastrous.

Companies may not yet realize it, but they need the extra edge a great brand story can give them in an ever more competitive marketplace. As Jensen forcefully argues in *The Dream Society*, today's most affluent, sought-after consumers have fewer pressing functional needs than ever before. Meanwhile, they also face far more offers in almost every product category than they could possibly need.

> *Nurturing a great brand story can create differentiation and add value, but it is especially helpful when differentiation and added value don't otherwise exist.*

The added bonus is that a storytelling approach to branding doesn't necessarily cost companies more than sticking with either of the two earlier eras of branding. Instead, it mostly means that they need to reorient their thinking so they can then refine their story-telling abilities.

Past assumptions have to be reexamined, starting with the old business equation anchored in the first era of branding. The old rational, utilitarian approach based on the views of Adam Smith and the neoclassical economists goes as follows:

$$SP \rightarrow R\,(e) = O/B$$

| Selling Points | Rational emotive | Offer Brand |

The new equation is instead:

$$SC \rightarrow E2\,(r) = S/B$$

| Sensory Clues | Emotive rational | Story Brand |

Now the branded story supercedes the literal offer and becomes the value proposition. A brand is no longer a platform for the rationally oriented offer.

That said, there's an exception: Early in the brand's life or development, its story is likely to be as much nonfiction as fiction. Early adopters or commodity buyers of its offer are likely to be taken by seeing the selling points together because the story isn't yet strong enough to reassure them that they are making the right choice.

> *Until the story builds up equity, both the rational and emotional approaches may need to be equally employed to carry the day.*

But, over time, a brand that provides any real added value paradoxically moves ever farther from nonfiction to fiction. It acquires emotional power that doesn't reside in facts.

Indeed, the brand story gains prominence because it can add depth by expanding the crucial sensory-emotive bandwidth. It becomes the shorthand by which the offer is known. Thus the story doesn't just frame the offer—in fact, it actually becomes more compelling than the offer will ever be.

That's why, for example, UPS has launched its Big Brown brand campaign. The company needed a brand story with some visibility, some pull, and some opportunity to promote customer affiliation with the brand. The highlighting of the color brown is based on the current UPS uniforms, which were originally tied to the brown uniforms worn by Pullman railroad car attendants because of their high professional standards. Are those the makings of an effective brand story for UPS?

Time will tell, but what is for certain is that the Big Brown campaign represents a concerted effort by UPS to move its brand classification from nonfiction to fiction in a single step.

Greater loyalty is the prize for any successful brand story effort.

Nevertheless, there's also danger in branding by stories, for the following reasons:

- *Nodding-heads syndrome*. By this, I mean that the brand story is too internalized. An effective brand story brings in new believers rather than just reassures existing believers. Therefore, one crucial test for the Big Brown campaign is whether the historical association with Pullman

(continued)

attendants resonates with anyone outside the company ranks.

- *Freezer-burn syndrome*. The brand story must evolve over time and with the times. If not, it risks becoming outdated. A good brand story keeps its core story line alive, but it also evolves and elaborates on the original story to provide what's crucially needed for the brand to remain relevant. Consider McDonald's: Given the greater emphasis currently being placed on eating healthy foods, it will likely respond with new offers. It will need to attend carefully to both any new offers and to the story that supports its response to this challenge.

- *Exposed-puppeteer syndrome*. The company as brand storyteller is like a puppeteer who must not let the audience see the puppet strings. You can't let the audience perceive or even think that you're manipulating it. Martha Stewart's alleged insider stock trading risks blowing up her carefully cultivated brand story because in effect a criminal investigation means the suspension of belief in her story—which is replaced by disbelief in the storyteller.

All three of these risks are eventually fatal to a brand, but the exposed-puppeteer syndrome brings brand death first. Here's why: While people lie to others and to themselves most of all, they still want to be sold fiction that they can consciously rationalize as nonfiction. They want the romance, but they also want the appearance of truth so that they can feel justified in investing more emotionally in a brand and find it to be of greater value than its net worth in rational terms.

Therefore, hide the puppet strings; otherwise, the magic will evaporate. And not slowly, but in an instant it will all come crashing down, story and offer alike.

If you can avoid these three syndromes, however, a brand story approach greatly benefits a company. With a great story, the senses and the emotions get engaged. The consumer is there for you. The further consumers are able to progress along the scale from nonfiction to fiction, the more commitment is generated. The price point is no longer the primary consideration because the consumer has internalized the value of the brand. You're in the sweet spot of delivering on Smith's view of the brand, only without really having to deliver any superior rationally-oriented benefits anymore.

The audience can't and won't hug a corporate giant. But it can and will emotionally hug a good storyteller.

Deeper Story Lines

Like the way a good player lights up a pinball machine, a strong brand story dynamically links its elements, thereby building a brand's deeper, nonrational power. A company really scores big with its brand story by tapping into a pair of deeper, more fundamental story lines that precede it and can either enhance or limit its effectiveness.

The first of these deep story lines is also the more tactical in nature. It involves navigating each emotion's own story, its own dramatic plot, or what I call its *emotive script*. I discuss this in further detail in the next chapter. In essence, every emotion has an internal logic to how its script unfolds: from core instinct, to theme, enactment, and the purpose behind the action.[7]

Consider anger, for instance. The story line of this emotion is that we experience a barrier to a goal, think the barrier is unjustified, want to smash it, and punish the party responsible for putting it there. If a company can identify the emotional chemistry of consumers' reactions to a TV spot, product, or store setting, for instance, then it's also able to grasp the motivational drivers and predict the likely sales outcome. The advantage is obvious: Beyond knowing what does and doesn't work, the chance to develop more cost-effective tactics for channeling consumers in closer to the brand.

Meanwhile, on a more strategic, brand-story level, a company will also benefit from exploring the second avenue to deeper story lines. This route involves certain basic, even archetypal stories or patterns that help shape consumer responses. These story lines are derived from experiences that we have known as a species through history and are therefore likely to be in the collective unconscious.

The starting point for both of these avenues is in the field of evolutionary psychology, a discipline that unites cognitive science, evolutionary biology, and genetics. Its concepts can help a company better understand whether a brand story is in sync with how the human psyche categorizes the world.

The four key adaptive issues the species instinctively responds to consist of:

- *Social hierarchies*. We all have images and experiences rooted in our psyches to suggest that

(continued)

height—either physical or hierarchical—is likely
to be equated with more resources and growth.

- *Territoriality.* We seek vistas and refuge, while
avoiding entanglements that jeopardize our
safety.

- *Group identity.* We worry about acceptance; this
concern makes warm/cold, inside/outside imagery
powerful.

- *Temporality.* Given our own limited life spans, we
fear loss and favor the status quo unless sufficiently threatened or encouraged to change.[8]

By using these intrinsic story lines, a company can manage the
demands of globalization. There are still, of course, different markets,
people, cultures, history, and geography. A good brand story can address these distinctions by adding individual accent touches to the
story in every case. Meanwhile, a company can keep the basic story
the same and overcome cultural differences by planting the emotional roots of the brand in soil that is common to the entire species.

What are the building blocks, the formula, for creating a solid
brand story? The answer to that question is the focus of the following chapter.

Notes

1. Hans Christian Andersen, "The Emperor's New Clothes," in *Classics of Children's Literature,* 2d ed., ed. John W. Griffith and Charles H. Frey
(New York: Macmillan, 1987), 137–139.

2. B. Joseph Pine II and James H. Gilmore, *The Experience Economy: Work Is Theatre & Every Business a Stage* (Boston: Harvard Business School Press, 1999), 1–15; Rolf Jensen, *The Dream Society: How the Coming Shift from Information to Imagination Will Transform Your Business* (New York: McGraw-Hill, 1999), 6–19.

3. Sharon Lee, quoted in Charles Pappas, "Where It's At: Cool and How to Find It," *Advertising Age*, May 20: 2002, 16. Reprintd with permission. © Crain Communications, Inc.

4. Eric Schlosser, *Fast Food Nation* (New York: HarperCollins, 2002), 4.

5. Mark Twain, "Mark Twain Tells the Secrets of Novelists," in *Life As I Find It* (New York: Hanover House, 1961), 338.

6. Mark Twain, "Fenimore Cooper's Literary Offences," in *How To Tell a Story and Other Essays* (New York: Harper, 1904), 79–81.

7. The subsequent descriptions and analysis of emotions is based on a multitude of sources. Among the key sources are the following: P. A. Andersen and L. K. Guerrero, *Handbook of Communication and Emotion: Research, Theory, Application, and Contexts* (New York: Academic Press, 1998); Paul Ekman, "All Emotions Are Basic," in *The Nature of Emotion:Fundamental Questions*, ed. Paul Ekman and Richard J. Davidson (New York: Oxford University Press, 1997); Morris Holbrook, "Emotion in the Consumption Experience: Toward a New Model of the Human Consumer," in *The Role of Affect in Consumer Behavior*, ed. Robert A. Peterson, Wayne D. Hoyer, and William R. Wilson (Lexington, MA: Lexington Press, 1986), 37; Andrew Ortony, Gerald R. Clore, and Allan Collins, *The Cognitive Structure of Emotions* (Cambridge: Cambridge University Press, 1988); Robert Plutchik, "A General Psychoevolutionary Theory," in *Approaches to Emotion*, ed. Klaus R. Scherer and Paul Ekman (Hillsdale, NJ: Lawrence Erlbaum Associates, 1984), 200; Marsha L. Richins, "Measuring Emotions in the Consumption Experience," *Journal of Consumer Research* 24 (September 1997): 144; and Ira Rosemen, cited in Rosalind Picard, *Affective Computing* (Cambridge, MA: MIT Press, 1997), 207.

8. Robert Plutchik, *The Emotions* (New York: University Press of America, 1990), 61–63.

Powerful Brand Story Design

Creating a Narrative That Will Solidify Consumer Devotion

I know from personal experience that a brand story can lead to an inexplicable devotion on the part of consumers. As a kid, I formed an attachment to, of all things, the quirky little cartoony commercials that were selling Starkist tuna. You may remember them yourself. The story was nothing more than Charlie the Tuna, who spent time in the water. The tagline was: "Only the best tasting tuna get to be Starkist."

Simplistic? Yes. Effective? In my case, yes. Of the two leading brands, Starkist and Bumble Bee, I can tell you that I have never bought a can of Bumble Bee tuna.

I attribute my unwavering brand loyalty to childhood memories of watching the Starkist spots while nestled in the basement. Life was simpler then—there were no planes to catch, no meetings, speeches, and so on. Charlie was an extra friend with a big smile.

For better or worse, I'll remember Charlie (brought in by a fishhook) and the tagline for the rest of my life. In contrast, I remember nothing about Bumble Bee. It just never resonated with me the same way that Starkist did.

Charlie the Tuna may not be an incredibly complex character, but he was just enough to nudge me into being a customer, which is everything in business. That's the purpose of this chapter: to help companies develop stronger brand stories to sell more, using the techniques that storytellers have used for centuries.

Story Setting: Owning a Mental Landscape

A great story has to happen some place, whether the setting is realistic or completely imaginary. In Mark Twain's case, creating the setting for *The Adventures of Huckleberry Finn* meant transforming his hometown of Hannibal, Missouri, into a place called St. Petersburg.[1] Led by Twain's words, readers then picture the setting on their own.

For companies, creating a story setting or "country" usually involves a combination of both real-life sensory clues—like smells or tactile impressions available in products or stores—and image-type clues like the Allstate "good hands" imagery communicated over the air waves and through other media vehicles.

Think of Charlie the Tuna at home in the sea. Whether physical or conceptual in nature, these clues lie embedded in the various contact points by which we form our perceptions about a company.

The story setting or its country is a brand's home territory, its turf, the spot it occupies in consumers' minds. The makings of a story country range across marketing applications, including not only the design but also the packaging and promotion of an offer. As to the characters who inhabit the story country, they consist not only of the service staff but also the fashion models used by the company and even the target audience itself.

Sometimes the branded story country literally exists. At the Magic Kingdom in Walt Disney World, the various exotic locales include Frontierland, featuring Tom Sawyer Island. There's also Hershey, Pennsylvania, a place where the street lights are shaped like candy kisses, the streets are named Chocolate and Cocoa, and families can visit Hersheypark, a chocolate-themed amusement park.

At other times, the story country is more mythical, perhaps existing only in make-believe. A case in point is Ralph Lauren's advertising invocation of a *Great Gatsby*–like existence on Long Island's Gold Coast. But surely the most famous story country remains Marlboro Country, a land where the cowboys ride high and the actual product—cigarettes—doesn't often get shown. It's a safe place for smokers to go, and they're surrounded by fellow believers.

A strong story country does a lot for a company. It lures consumers, and it fends off enemies. Most of all, it provides a robust and strategically innovative route out of the dead zone of being seen as just a commodity.

Companies must find a mental landscape they can own, in which consumers enthusiastically want to live.

Harley-Davidson remains as good an example as any of how owning a piece of mental turf translates into sales. From the motorcycles to clothing and additional lifestyle accessories, Harley-Davidson has built a sphere for its customers to occupy. The holy land is the Sturgis rally, leading to photos of time well spent on your hog.

How can a company go about creating an optimal story country? The place to start is by remembering that the story country sets up the sensory clues. It launches the sense-feel-(think)-do model of consumer decision making. Those clues will drive the degree of emotional connection a brand can make with its target audience.

A company must scrupulously attend to the sensory clues being created, and it must choose land that has solid, long-term potential.

Rational factors may contribute to the value of the story country, but the following intuitive influences contribute more:

- *Sensory.* Are the clues sufficiently interesting to survive the hippocampus's filter? What's too bland won't register. Moreover, any clues that have already been used by rivals aren't likely to work because the mind prefers to classify things, and any overlap or confusion blocks that essential drive.

- *Emotional.* This speaks to the question about whether the property has curb appeal. By *curb appeal*, I mean that it has to feel right, like it could be home, or else the crucial ingredient of emotional dimensionality will never grow within the consumers' psyche.

A company must take the consumers' point of view. It must ask itself, "Is this mental turf that feels safe? Will it draw lots of traffic because it exists in the vicinity of people's needs and psychological sight lines?"

A successful story setting strategy must begin with sensory clues that connect with consumers on as much of a universal basis as possible. This approach enables a company to create a story with a wide emotional bandwidth.

Clues that address specific target audiences are fine—in fact, they can broaden and enrich the story setting. But there has to be an overall, unifying look and style to the story. The customized clues must support and never undercut or be at odds with the rest of the mental landscape being presented to consumers.

Associations: Building a Strong Network

The practice of corporate branding takes its name from the old English verb *baernan* (to burn) and refers to the burning of maker marks on barrels of liquor in Elizabethan England to distinguish them from those of rival no-name distillers. Branding quite literally began as the act of burning into place a company's name as a kind of memory stamp.

Today, branding is still about establishing and protecting a company's market position, but now the focus has grown in scope and importance. Branding has moved beyond merely marketing the product. It now focuses on creating an overarching, meaningful brand story to increase the depth and dimensionality of the offer.

The drive to sear one's name into consumers' memories—and hearts—has found support from science because the latest findings show that once a network of associations gets started, building on that network is the easiest, most effective way to build lasting loy-alty. Companies that can create an enduring sensory-emotive con-nection are in luck. They have their branded film footage running in the magic camera of perceptions and memories that unfold inside our heads.

The simple truth is that stories contain knowledge. A com-pany can build our trust and affection by planting inside of us an emotional spark, then repeating and enhancing this initial experience. In other words, past associations serve as a net for catching new ones.

Thus, the problem with New Coke was that it took what we had already internalized in our brains and contradicted that sense of loy-alty. When a story lives and breathes and is of interest to us, we want to replay it in our heads. We want to weave emotional con-nections around it. In a phrase, we want to own the story. We may even want to elaborate on it, like a good fishing story in which over the years the size of the fish keeps getting bigger.

Consumers want to take a general story and personalize it. Successful brand stories make their associations work in such a manner that they invite us to become fellow storytellers.

In earlier eras, branding meant being happy just to create a co-hesive company image, but that's no longer enough. The new era of experiential branding requires a company to create an emotional aura around itself. By going deeper and wider, a company can hold off the competition and get closer to consumers.

The degree to which there's a quality catch of such items as imagery, jingles, memories, and concepts by which we connect to a company indicates whether intimacy is being created. The differences between creating a story country versus lasting associations as well as between product versus brand associations clarify the picture.

In essence, the story country versus the associations surrounding it is the same as content versus context. A company's story country is something consumers can actively visualize and experience. Its content involves perceptual imagery, sensory clues. In contrast, associations are invisible: the mental attributes we extrapolate from the clues and attribute to the brand. They're the context, the stakes hidden in the ground that mark the outer reaches of the story country.

The other distinction—offer versus brand story associations—is equally crucial. If most of the associations reside merely on a functional, features-driven offer level, then the story is likely to be weak and its emotive power is likely to be absent.

> Think about how countries evoke patriotism:
>
> - They confront the challenge of creating within their constituencies a sense of identification so strong that they feel like they belong to something larger than themselves.
>
> - They attempt to evoke something that puts citizens inside the fence, protected against the outer world.
>
> - They want to create a feeling that puts citizens within the gravitational pull of the entity, circling in a perpetual, self-reinforcing emotional orbit.
>
> *(continued)*

> • The goal is to generate a web of associations that's unconsciously so powerful that a viable, ongoing relationship is formed.

In the United States, we have specific items that have graduated to the level of becoming patriotic associations: among them, the flag, the Pledge of Allegiance, the founding fathers, Mount Rushmore (see Figure 6.1), and the White House. With a brand, a company must follow suit. It needs to identify and nurture the clues that instill the brand's basic values and ideology.

Figure 6.1 This shrine to democracy was originally meant to showcase local Western heroes like Lewis and Clark and Kit Carson. But by its completion in 1941, the 60-foot-tall faces of four of our leading presidents were what chiseler extraordinaire Gutzon Borglum had sculpted to honor America, creating an extraordinary signature clue that brands the Black Hills as American.

In strategic terms, the need to create patriotism means that a company must have a flag—not just a logo but a strong sensory-emotive signature clue—that serves as the rallying cry for the brand. It must lay claim to unique territory in consumers' heads, as well as in their hearts, setting off feelings that become richer as a brand matures along with us.

> *The objective in creating the brand story is to form associative, emotional links that wouldn't otherwise survive rational scrutiny. They should lie so deep, so internalized, that consumers accept them without question.*

Personality: Creating a Distinct Connection

Besides a setting, another element any story must have is characterization. Stories have people in them. Yet it's amazing how often companies neglect this basic piece of the puzzle by creating a brand personality that's essentially faceless or anonymous. In the new era of experiential branding and story design, this failure is fatal. The companies that get there first by creating a viable, engaging personality will enjoy a huge advantage over the laggards.

What does having a personality mean? Its usage stems from the Latin term *persona*, referring to the masks worn by actors in early drama. But in the modern business world, *personality* refers to a set of predictable behaviors by which consumers will recognize a company when they look behind any mask, any corporate spin.

One of the key purposes of a brand is, of course, to serve as a guarantee.

> *The establishment of reliable, positive company traits provides a supporting framework for the offer. It puts the consumer at ease by bringing otherwise isolated, disparate images together in a single enduring snapshot of the company.*

A strong consistent profile serves as a quick signpost that makes life easier by helping us know with whom we're dealing. A company that keeps changing traits isn't somebody we're going to trust to act on our behalf in the marketplace. Think of Kmart, schizophrenically veering between the Blue Light Special—indicative of a down-market retailer—and the Martha Stewart products, which aim for a more upscale consumer.

Although a set of consistent, reassuring traits enables trust, reaching that point is really just the cost of entry in a branding strategy game in which the stakes keep getting higher. Knowing how a company is likely to act in any given situation speaks more to the functional offer level than it does to creating a true brand story personality.

A sense of security that invokes only a company's identity isn't enough. An identity must achieve the following:

- It must do more than merely eliciting recognition—it must conjure up not only consumer acceptance but also enthusiasm and loyalty. The business world would do well to remember that it's personality that can win people over.

- How consumers characterize or personify a company's traits matters because nothing generates as

(continued)

> much emotion as interacting with others, be it a
> person or a company.
>
> - A distinctive brand personality helps differenti-
>   ate a company, and companies should use that
>   fact to their advantage.

People are fascinated by what sensory clues reveal about other people's personalities. The same can hold true in business. If we sense a warm, attractive brand personality, we'll feel more intimately attached and we'll want to stay in touch.

A case in point is Geek Squad. This company is a small story that is becoming a bigger story about how to leverage an engaging brand personality. This 24-hour residential computer service business (in selected cities) makes being nerdy hip.[2] "Special agents" (technology experts) dress in black pants and ties, white socks and shirts, and drive around in black-and-white Volkswagen Beetles known as Geekmobiles, on their way to the rescue of consumers experiencing difficulties with their computers. This brand is memorable and fun.

Indeed, the right personality creates empathy and commitment. Now more than ever before, companies need to establish the kind of brand profile that can help them gain new customers, strengthen their bonds with existing customers, and serve as brand equity to help ward off problems when they arise.

Plot: Linking Consumer Needs and Story Type

Besides setting and characters, the other main element that a story needs to have is a plot. Plot involves movement and change. In literature, the plot is often talked about in terms of a conflict between

people and themselves, others, or forces like nature or political systems. In business the notion of plot is at once both easier to get a
handle on yet subtle and complex.

Plot addresses the conflict inherent in any brand story between
a customer's needs and a company's ability to satisfy them. Creating
a compelling plot can be challenging—the difficulty lies in the act
of measuring the general level of consumer "satisfaction" in regard
to every story country touch point (promotion, product, people, or
place clue). Creating a plot is also challenging because there's pressure to make plot incorporate every association, every character or
corporate personality trait, and so on.

However, remember that consumers are seeking to simplify the
world to enable quick decisions—not unlike the way the amygdala
responds on first blush along the low road of decision making.
Whether it's done consciously or not, consumers classify everything,
including satisfaction potential.

For the purposes of brand story plot, two categories of
possible classification are the most pertinent: *consumer needs* and what I call the *brand story type* (the
way consumers define the genre or nature of the
brand and its size or intensity).

Together, consumer needs and story type outline the dynamics and flavor of the customer–brand
relationship and the degree to which a satisfying
outcome is likely. They also suggest whether the
offer and the brand are in sync. In other words, are
the offer and the brand helping or hurting each
other?

Effective Needs Linkage: Going Up a Down Escalator

Determining the emotional basis for the customer–brand relationship starts with consumer needs. There are many ways to analyze them. It's tempting to stay close to the surface and emphasize a rational, utilitarian distinction between functional, must-have needs or differentiating, ideal-value needs, for instance—or even to step it up a notch and distinguish between basic, category, and differentiating needs.

The greatest value is to return to a more basic level and explore the fundamental mind/body needs that apply universally. To drive up sales, a company's focus on consumer needs must take the down escalator to a basic level instead.

There are two parts to the strategy: The first is that to adhere to psychologist Abraham Maslow's famous hierarchy of needs theory, a company must start by addressing consumers' basic, deficiency type needs. The lowest four ascending rungs—physical, safety, social, and esteem—are all deficiency needs. Self-actualization sits on top as the one and only positive, "surplus" need (see Figure 6.2).[3]

According to Maslow, the lowest-level need will remain the consumer's motivational driver—until satisfied—at which point the next highest rung becomes the focal point. If higher needs aren't met, a consumer will return to the lower needs as the primary driver of brand loyalty.

A company that seeks to form an optimal connection with consumers must understand that not all needs are of equal psychological intensity. In fact, the greatest power lies at the most basic level (see Figure 6.3).

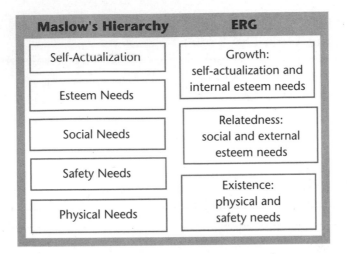

Figure 6.2 Maslow's Hierarchy of Needs and the ERG Theory

Recently, Clayton Alderfer of Yale University has offered an ERG (existence, relatedness, growth) theory that modifies Maslow's model. ERG allows for needs to be met simultaneously and has fewer rungs on the ladder.[4]

These models help a company envision its offer by understanding where along the hierarchy it is creating a connection with the target audience. Exploring the type of needs consumers associate with a company's offer provides a fresh and deeper look at what business a company is in, beyond the categories listed in *Fortune's* annual ranking of the top 500 companies.

You might think you're selling insurance, but depending on the policy type and the target audience's social-economic profile, you could be, for instance, potentially fulfilling a lower-level physical need to

(continued)

The Role of Products in Our Daily Lives

Product Example	Role / Definition	Emotionality	Involvement
Furniture, appliances	Background/ part of setting	Prop for events	Very low
Greeting cards, souvenirs	Mediator/ prompts interaction	Focal point for interactions	Moderate-low
Cosmetics, food, beverages	Enhancement/ facilitates performance	Influences success	Moderate-high
Clothing, home decorations	Self-expression self-image	Influences self-esteem	High
Cars, electronic equipment	Object/ invested in	Substitute for relationships	Very high

In developing, designing, and marketing a product, a company will want to investigate carefully which role or roles are viable for the product in question.

• Is the product merely background, just part of the scene, props on the stage where important events occur in our life?
• A mediator—can it bridge a gap between people? Does it initiate or reaffirm an interpersonal relationship?
• As enhancement—does it improve the social interaction by lifting the consumer's ability to perform a function?
• As self-expression—does the product define us to ourselves and to others, serving as an indication of self-esteem?
• As object—does the product become the object of emotions, often as a substitute for human relationships or for its sensory value?

Figure 6.3 The Role of Products in Our Daily Lives. (Reprinted with permission from Rowan Littlefield from Peterson, Hoyer, and Wilson, eds., *The Role of Affect in Consumer Behavior* [Lanham, MD: Lexington Books, 1986], p. 123.)

put food on the table in case a parent dies. Alternatively, you could be fulfilling a higher social need to prove to one's family and friends that by buying insurance one is a prudent planner. Orientations toward these needs mean that your brand story will be vastly different for each one, with unique clues so that the offer and brand don't get misaligned.

The second part of the down-escalator strategy involves the opportunity for a company not only to address needs but also to recognize and leverage the potency of consumers' fears.

Fear motivates most people at least as much as does the hope of having a need realized. But given the fight-or-flight tendency, invoking fear can set off retreat. After all, we're hard-wired through evolution to be wary of threats that endanger our survival. Therefore, although we hear bad news the loudest, we also readily engage in avoidance behavior by preferring to figuratively kill the messenger. In business, a company can't afford to get killed in the short term only to be recognized as a prophet years later.

The recourse is to avoid stating the fear aloud. Instead, a company should let the visuals and other sensory clues suggest the fear in such a way that it's as if consumers discover it on their own and internalize it. Then it's *their* fear—rather than a threat the company exploited. (In Chapter 8, I discuss how companies can appeal to other psychological needs that are deeply ingrained in all humans.)

Effective Story Type: A Universal Imprint

To bring the customer–brand relationship into better focus, the brand story also rewards analysis. One variable is the story type, categories like those used by video rental stores to sort movies as action, drama, science fiction, and so on.

The truth is that to achieve great brand story equity, a company must ride on the coattails of story types that already have mind share throughout the world's markets.[5] After all, among all literature ever written from mythology, fairy tales, and the ancient classics to Harlequin romances, there are really only a handful of story types. With each story type, there are some very well-established expectations about the kind of plot, mood, and theme that will predominate.

The brand story type in strategic business terms is the outer ring around the story's set of associations, or the meta-context. It frames the associative context that in turn frames the story's content—its sensory clues. Case in point: consider Microsoft. Once upon a time, Bill Gates was a challenger. He was the upstart inventor that IBM rejected as a would-be business partner. In those days, Gates was like Luke Skywalker wielding a light saber in *Star Wars*, or David using a slingshot against the giant Goliath in the Bible.

Today, thanks to Microsoft's unprecedented success, Gates is now the giant. Because of his success, the way Microsoft evolves its story has to be very carefully handled. Remember: Once this story gets established in the hearts and minds of consumers, a brand's deep, universal story type isn't easily dislodged.

As to the second variable, story size matters: large, medium, or small. In other words, how strong is the story? How well does it capture our imagination and draw us toward the brand? Is it drab and small, or powerful, like Microsoft's story?

Together, story type and size indicate how the target audience intuitively perceives a company's style, mood, and energy level. Those twin dynamics of type and size should fit the nature of the offer and also fit the emotional dynamics of whatever universal needs the offer is really attempting to fulfill. The degree to which everything aligns will clarify whether the consumer–brand relationship is on track.

Theme: Strategizing an Effective Code

The "title" of the brand story combines the company's and the product's name. It has power to the extent that either name can create deep or intriguing associations in consumers' hearts and minds. The story's theme—the deep-down, sensory-emotive value proposition—is subtler. It requires a strategy beyond just finding the best name for an offer.

One way to understand a brand story theme is to define it in negative terms—to explain what it *isn't*. Crafting the story theme isn't just the creation of a mission statement. That string of buzzwords and platitudes is most often just a company talking to itself. In addition, the theme is often equated with a transient tagline, a phrase that gets discarded when the next advertising campaign comes along.

On the contrary, story theme is best approached in Walt Disney's terms. As a cartoonist used to building his narrative frame by frame, Walt brought comic strips, film, and his cinematically oriented theme parks together whenever he would ask his Imagineers, "What's the end frame?"[6]

By "end frame," Walt meant that he wanted to know the emotional pay-off for a ride or any experience a guest might have within the theme park. The reason he objected to employees driving a truck through Frontierland during park hours, for instance, is that the motor vehicle was a twentieth-century invention. Its presence would clash with a movie set in the Wild West, thus imperiling not only the emotional pay-off for the guests but also the park's theme of enchantment. To see a truck was to break the spell and destroy the magic, and the same would be true if the seediness that doomed Coney Island crept into the theme park, replacing magic with safety concerns.

As Walt would have argued, in devising a theme, it's important not to rely on using an old-fashioned positioning grid—you know the type, with the two key rationally oriented variables that reflect how a consumer supposedly chooses between options, one of which is price. This sort of approach is out of touch with what science now tells us about how consumers actually choose their brands. Such an approach is abstract—and it lacks an emotional kick.

A stronger, more grounded approach is to create a short code consisting of either a phrase or separate words that together embody the essence of the sensory-emotive connection being forged with consumers.

A good code provides a trio of advantages:

- First, it's more intimate than the usual positioning statement, emphasizing emotional benefits that won't soon become obsolete.

- Second, it offers specific guidance for how to shape the sensory clues that form the basis of experiential branding.

(continued)

> - Finally, its greater dimensionality provides the opportunity to break, block, or override the code of rival companies. In story terms, it creates the chance to be the leader, the protagonist of a category.

A case in point is Barnes & Noble, with a theme of being a third place—neither home nor office. In an age of hustle and bustle, this bookseller provides soft, oversized chairs to sink into—a refuge in which we can cultivate our minds and rest both body and soul (see Figure 6.4).

Whatever the thematic code proves to be, a company's CEO and the brand managers need to remember that most often a company's brand story writes itself.

The process organically unfolds, over time, and the story gains much of its power from the fact that it happens on a largely intuitive, even unconscious basis. Therefore, as leaders their job is to recognize, protect, and nurture the company's ability to tap into the deepest or main channel. The main channel always lies in enhancing consumers' emotional commitment to the brand story and its theme, which is what managing a brand is really about.

Creative Brief as Story Research Tool

To create a strong brand story, a company needs to know whether its strategy and executions are on target. I believe that science and

Figure 6.4 As "Booksellers Since 1873," Barnes & Noble's chairs are its signature clue. This defining detail reflects the company's style positioning, which includes book signage that echoes the wallpaper designs of the Victorian artist William Morris, a member of the pre-Raphaelite movement that rebelled against the gray, dehumanizing elements of the Industrial Revolution. (Printed with permission from Barnes & Noble, Inc.)

storytelling combine to offer the best one-two punch—that is, marketers can use these tools to create a story that appeals to the innate desires within every human. The new scientific findings tell us about the dominant role of the unconscious and of the sensory-emotive connection. Meanwhile, storytelling is full of mythological power and has in its tool kit the means of helping enact that connection.

One way to verify the robust health of the brand story is to learn if enough consumer insights exist to develop a solid creative brief.

You can test your story by asking questions like the following:

- What images and words are working?
- What changes should the creative director make?
- What changes should the product manager make?
- Where's the story now?
- Where should it be?
- How will it get there?

These questions require answers available to brand directors who must act as skilled doctors, very carefully performing the required work. Their goal should always be to extend and enhance the life of an already existing, organically developed brand story.

Thus, the brand directors' first priority is to understand what already exists. What works, and what doesn't? What material will they be adjusting? Those are questions that must be answered to heighten the odds of success. Only by knowing what lies closest to the heart of the brand can the crucial brand story elements be protected well enough.

A good brand story "surgeon" grasps the reality that there isn't much room in which to operate. Inside the chest cavity of any company's brand story, everything relates to everything else.

The temptation with any brand surgery is to start anew, but the impulse, though possibly on target, must be scrutinized. Otherwise, the outcome may prove to be like what happened to Izod. Eager for more sales, the company began to sell its clothing in brand outlets. But the aura of exclusivity was at odds with a product now available more cheaply, and the brand faltered.

With any brand story operation, executives and brand managers must avoid overreaching or challenging the basic thematic premise of the story. The surest way to kill a brand story is to interject something foreign into it, which it rejects, while leaving a void. Figure 6.5 offers a review of the important parts of a brand story.

Here are some vital signs for a brand story:

Story Setting

- How strong is the story country?
- What clues best fortify it?
- How well do the story country and its clues perform for consumers?

Remember that the traditional, verbal research tools are the least appropriate given the major role that often unconscious, sensory perceptions and the resulting emotional triggers play in consumers' decision-making process. A mind/body approach should ideally be used to test the strength of the story country, but if not, then picture sorts or other visually oriented techniques may help gauge how well the sensory clues perform.

Key Brand Story Design Elements	
Settings	Story country and associations
Characters	Traits that personify the company, its rivals, and possibly: target audiences, the offer, sector, and individual advertising campaigns
Plot	The conflict resolution involving consumer needs vis-à-vis the offer and the dynamics of the brand story type/size
Title	Name of the company and its branded offer
Theme	Value proposition and positioning, as expressed through a positioning code and enacted by the design brief

Figure 6.5 Key Brand Story Design Elements

Associations

- What's the core concept, and is it unique?
- What perceptions are owned by rivals or else are too functional and generic?

Anything too vague or flat won't help create a story country capable of defending itself. To analyze associations (like Crest owning the term *anti-cavity*), David Aaker and others provide worthy models.[7]

Traits

- Is the brand personality attractive?
- Where are its vulnerabilities?

(continued)

- Is it stronger or weaker than those of rivals?

- What role models does it suggest?

To assess a company's character profile or how the offer is perceived in human terms, one option rises above the rest: The top psychology model for assessing personalities belongs to the research team of P. T. Costa, Jr. and R. R. McCrae.[8] Their "big five" factors break personality down into the dimensions of extroversion, conscientiousness, openness, agreeableness, and negative emotionality (neuroticism). Again and again in tests, the big five model has proven best able to encompass the variability of character.

Needs

- What are the potential emotional triggers?

- What do consumers want to attain and avoid?

- What are they really buying from the company?

Needs, wants, and fears have to be investigated at a level that opens new ways of seeing the offer's deeper, intrinsic mind/body value. Here Maslow's hierarchy or a version thereof remains the strongest option.

Story Type

- Does the story type match up well with the offer and needs?

- What's the story's emotional energy level?

- What kind of lifestyle does it signify?

These issues help define how well the company and its offer combine, whether they form a cohesive unit or are at odds with one another and with the target audience's sensory-emotive chemistry. The goal is to have a story type that puts a halo around the offer. An investigation of literary genres, mythology, and Jung's archetypes offers the best bet for building an analytical platform involving comedy, tragedy, and other types of stories.

Ultimately, the creative brief must serve two purposes: The first is to guard the brand story's integrity and its ability to inspire trust. The audience must stay caught up in the story's sensory-emotive flow; anything that causes consumers to abandon their willing suspension of disbelief is a disaster from which long-term recovery is doubtful.

Second, the creative brief needs to take the story where the greatest potential exists. A brand story is about establishing greater emotional bandwidth—more power, depth, and breadth. The strongest approach uses the raw materials hard-wired into us through evolution and takes them globally. As I explain in the next chapter, marketers can use the brand story to create positioning for products that speaks to human needs and desires that are both universal and innate.

Notes

1. Mark Twain, *The Adventures of Huckleberry Finn* (New York: Blue Unicorn, 1998).

2. Sherri Cruz, "Best Buy and Geek Squad Join Forces," *Minneapolis Star-Tribune*, October 25, 2002, pp. D1, D4.

3. Abraham Maslow, *Motivation and Personality* (New York: Harper, 1954).

4. Clayton Alderfer, "ERG Theory," online document available at http://www.netmba.com.

5. Margaret Mark, and Carol S. Pearson, *The Hero and the Outlaw: Building Extraordinary Brands Through the Power of Archetypes* (New York: McGraw-Hill, 2001), 31.

6. Kathy Merlock Jackson, *Walt Disney* (Westport, CT: Greenwood, 1993).

7. David A. Aaker, *Brand Leadership* (New York: Free Press, 2000).

8. Pierce J. Howard, *The Owner's Manual for the Brain* (New York: Bard Press, 2000), 411–432.

Emotional Positioning

How to Sell Your Products Based on Their Emotional Resonance

From what I've covered so far, you know that consumers evaluate an offer in three seconds or less. This is the common length of time in which people develop an emotional response; thus, we have three seconds in which to roll into action. Those three seconds will go a long way toward determining a company's market share, and they're largely predicated on sensory clues for tipping the scales in our favor. These sensory clues are often left to outsiders or junior-level subordinates to determine, but as I've argued, they're far too potent to leave to chance.

In this chapter, I'll bring more strategic depth to offer positioning by plugging in sensory-emotive considerations to a degree that most companies have previously failed to reach. The previous chapters have provided scientific findings, top 10 rules, specific research tools (biofeedback, facial coding) and a methodology (branding as story design), all of which take time to master as well as equipment and training.

Naturally, you want something you can use *right now,* today, as a means of growing market share, brand loyalty, and profits. Thus, this chapter and the next two provide a field guide of some essential building blocks that you can plug in and work with immediately. My goal is to provide a means of diagnosing a strategy and being able to evaluate the suitability of creative output.

These building blocks won't bust your budget. They won't cost extra money to implement, and they're multipliers. They will offer more impact for a marketing dollar through a better fit with consumers and a better position against competitors—in other words, an edge—as soon as you use them.

To build a more valuable, robust, and sustainable offer positioning, you will need to engage in analysis, revisions, and synergies involving these elements:

- *Sensory metaphors.* In other words, basic perceptual categories by which people define the world.

- *Emotive scripts.* The story line for each of the key emotions consumers experience. I'll discuss this concept in further detail in the next chapter.

- *Primitive needs.* Scientists have identified six essential, universal human motivations, drawn from evolutionary psychology. I'll show you how to make these drives and desires work in your favor.

As I will show, these building blocks are pertinent whether you're doing an audit of your company's own creative output, a competitive sector analysis, or a gap analysis involving customer versus employee perceptions. I'll also discuss the biological gender gap differences in how men and women relate to the various elements.

In this chapter, I'll give you thumbnail sketches of the essential metaphors, emotions, and needs that may apply to your company's offer positioning. In the Chapter 8 I'll bring those elements together—aligning them into combinations that build positioning, even according to specific business sectors.

A World of Sensory Metaphors

Before we can get to the actual sensory metaphors, there are two questions worth answering:

- What exactly *are* sensory metaphors?
- Why should anyone in business care about them?

To define a metaphor is relatively easy. Metaphors are comparisons—they say one thing in terms of another. Some common metaphors would be complimenting someone's "sapphire eyes," referring to a hard-working person as a "busy bee," and "like sand in the hourglass go the days of our lives."

As you can see from these examples, metaphors are tied to the physical world. They're sensory. The comparisons they involve are implicit and intuitive in nature.

Sensory metaphors are important to companies and to their marketing departments in particular because common, primary metaphors reflect how consumers perceive the world and make connections.

To achieve a deeper, richer connection with consumers, sensory metaphors are valuable because they accomplish the following:

- *Provide a handle.* Sensory metaphors involve a correlation we have experienced so often that the link has become automatic. The key metaphors reveal how our minds inevitably categorize the world to make quick sense of it.

- *Access the unconscious.* Sensory metaphors acknowledge and access the inexpressible—what we already know, and what works so well that it's effectively invisible to us, like the ground we walk on every day.

- *Speak in images.* These metaphors express in visual or other sensory terms the 80 percent of communication that is nonverbal. Because we think in images, not words, sensory metaphors achieve more connectedness.

- *Express our feelings.* Sensory metaphors indicate how people feel about their perceptual experiences. They reveal an emotional response and understanding as consumers encounter the world.

To date, very few companies have gone down this road. One exception is Allstate Insurance, with its famous "You're in good hands" slogan. Another is Campbell's Soup with "Mmm Mmm Good." These two companies initialized taglines that became metaphors for their respective offers. By showing us a pair of hands, palms up, Allstate is really saying that they are there to hold us, protect us, look out for our interests. Meanwhile, Campbell's Soup's very phonetic tagline hearkens back to the smell, taste, and touch sensations that come from eating warm bowls of soup.

The value of these two sensory metaphors is phenomenal. The barrier to entry that well-crafted metaphors create for competitors is even more impressive. All of this is accomplished at no greater cost than that of using weak, inappropriate metaphors—or none at all.

Using Color

The human eye can see millions of colors. They affect us based on how light waves absorbed by the retina turn into nerve impulses. The impulses are sent to the brain, which then interprets them as messages to either speed up or slow down the systems in the body.

In other words, like the other fundamental sensory metaphors I'll soon address, the impact of color involves a biological basis that turns into an emotional response.

Let's look at some key colors in a little greater depth:

- *Blue* has a short wavelength, and has been shown to lower blood pressure, pulse, and respiration rates. (Color preference studies indicate that blue is a universally preferred color.)

- *Red,* in contrast, is the most stimulating color, has a long wavelength, and attracts the eye faster than any other color. (In preference studies, red draws the hot-blooded crowd and comes in second to blue.)

- *Yellow* is in the middle of the wavelengths detectable by the human eye. It is the brightest color and easily attracts attention

but is also the most tiring color because of the excessive stimulation it causes. (In preference studies, yellow typically comes in
last in preference.)

Overall, each color behaves in one of three basic
ways:

- Active;
- Passive;
- Neutral.

Active colors are warm and include red, purple,
and orange. These colors exude confidence and often
inspire positive feelings. Passive, cool colors like blue
and green pacify and restore. Finally, neutral colors
include beige, gray, white, and taupe. Neutral colors
send a restful message to your brain and are capable of
reducing stress.

With millions of color options to select from, how well do companies do in choosing colors based on the symbolic, associative, and
physical reactions consumers have to them? Let's look for example
at how the various rental car agencies are differentiated by their primary corporate color: Hertz is yellow, Avis is red, National is green,
and so on. Avis's use of red—an active color that suggests boldness
plus movement—reinforces the "we try harder" slogan. The yellow
and black Hertz identifier communicates alertness with an authori-
tative edge. National, on the other hand, takes a less energetic but

more comforting stance: Green is the most restful and soothing color for the human eye.

Color is received more easily than form and is immediate (without need of translation). In effect, colors enable quick, memorable identification by harried travelers. How well do these colors relate to the nature of the offer? How do they indicate the *unique* personality or character of the respective companies?

Visually Oriented Sensory Metaphors

Color is the first stage of creating sensory metaphors for most companies because it's the level most readily known, understood, and accepted. For example, most people realize that, for instance, the color red is often associated with passion, love, and danger.

Color serves as a metaphor because you can say something about a company and its offer simply with the color scheme that gets employed.

Color is by no means the only visually oriented sensory metaphor that companies can and should use to market their branded offers more effectively. By my count, there are 27 common sensory metaphors— of which all but 6 are primarily or at least partially related to visual perceptions.

Why so many visually oriented sensory metaphors? There are two excellent reasons: The first is that, as a species, humans are very visually oriented. In fact, it's been estimated that learning is 83 percent visual, 11 percent auditory, 3.5 percent smell, 1.5 percent touch, and 1 percent taste. The other nonvisual senses may create a stronger reaction because they are less commonly used and people are in more immediate, intimate physical proximity to a stimulus when they can use them. The fact that they get used more rarely and in close-up situations gives them added kick.

In the centuries since human beings began to walk upright, there's no question that we comprehend the world most readily and frequently through our eyes instead of our ears, nose, fingers, or tongue.

This brings me to the second reason why visually oriented metaphors predominate: Sight is how we most often begin the act of comprehension. We spot something around us (and maybe we hear it, too). But only if the distance narrows—and intimacy exists—will we touch, smell, and taste an object.

Sight is our primary information-gathering mode.

To discuss the 27 common sensory metaphors, I've decided to concentrate on the 21 that are primarily or at least partially related to visual perceptions. In my introduction, I'll include a business example to illustrate how and why a particular metaphor is or isn't working in a specific print ad or TV spot.

Entirely Visual Sensory Metaphors

There are only two sensory metaphors that are entirely visual in nature. Of these, the first one is closely tied to the use of color, particularly color value:

Light/Dark (Dim/Bright)

Throughout history, people have learned to associate light with vision—and vision with empowering, protective knowledge.

To be in the dark puts humans in risk mode. We're ill at ease in a pitch-black room because our primary sense has been cut off. We depend on what our eyes see to appraise our surroundings.

Metaphorically, evolution has taught us that light is safety, just as knowledge is seeing ("I see what you mean"). In contrast, darkness is often danger—in the same way that ignorance is equated with an inability to see (as in "a blind spot"). Of course, darkness can have its positive side, too. It can be alluring, a time for romance or mystery—and it can represent a chance to escape from everyday pressures.

In general, as a species humans are drawn more to light because it's comforting, safer, and, in relation to daytime and the sun, signals a greater opportunity for warmth (another of the sensory metaphors).

Example: A Bacardi rum print ad makes appropriate use of this metaphor by emphasizing darkness as danger and, therefore, excitement. The ad shows a young man watched by others as he break-dances. His white pants legs are up in the air, in a split. His head is down into the darkness of the dance floor, which has the Bacardi bat logo embossed on it. "Bacardi by night" in black type echoes the mood of the photo. The ad is dangerous and thrilling.

Dirty/Clean

As my company's research into human needs discovered (to my surprise), cleanliness is among the absolutely most important, appealing needs to satisfy—well ahead of more glamorous options like intimacy, recognition, and entertainment.

The reason for this lies in basic biology. At issue here is the species' instinctive, self-protecting desire to avoid anything that might be *poisonous*. By way of analogy, think of fresh meat versus carrion. (Don't we regard vultures that prey on rotting carcasses as dirty, ugly birds?) We want a safe, hospitable environment, in part because (like the related metaphor of chaotic/orderly) dirty/clean invokes basic survival concerns involving health, vitality, security, and efficiency.

Example: A Bounty paper towels ad makes good use of this metaphor by showing rolls of paper towels on shelves alongside a collection of white ceramic pottery pieces. What's implied is that Bounty's ability to deliver cleanliness is as valuable as these other crafted works. In warding off the unholy trinity of dirt, disease, and danger, Bounty proves its worth by delivering the very rich psychological territory of reassurance.

Visual and Tactile Sensory Metaphors

There are 11 sensory metaphors that can apply to both sight and touch. I consider them to be more visually oriented metaphors, however, not only because the visual "reading" typically happens before touch but also because the visual application of the metaphor tends to predominate.

Big/Small
Tall/Short

The cliché is that size matters, and it's often true. Usually, the assumption is that bigger is considered to be better; largely, that is also often true up to a certain point. Clearly many Americans favor large sizes—we're buying "starter castles" to live in, and big SUVs to drive. Supersizing is no longer just a meal option, it's a way of life.

Big/small is a major sensory metaphor because it carries many implications. When something is physically larger, we also tend to attach other emotionally tinged psychological attributes to it. The reasons for the general bias in favor of big things include the following:

- In biological terms, bigger tends to suggest strength, protection, and security—in a word, invulnerability. We think a bigger watchdog provides more safety.

- Larger things are often seen as more important. To say, "Tomorrow is a big day," gives it substance.

- Size suggests status, wealth, and abundance. In effect, *big* serves as a metaphor for the expectation of getting more.

- Size (as in height) can convey the impression of being big and bold—a leader. It impresses.

- Size can mean intimacy. In a movie, for instance, a person or object shot close-up is larger. Being close can increase interest and importance because it signals intimacy, intensity, and engagement.

At the same time, however, bigger isn't always better. To be too big is to dwarf others, creating a disparity that can make everyone uncomfortable. To be too big suggests the image of Frankenstein stumbling through the woods. Likewise, if something or somebody is too big, as in too close up, we might feel threatened and intimidated.

Particularly if it's an unwelcome advance from someone or something that's big, we feel like our personal space is being violated.

The evaluation of size doesn't revolve entirely around the pluses and minuses of being big. Although being small, as in small-minded, is clearly bad, there can also be plenty of advantages to being small. For instance, there's the cliché that "big gifts come in little packages."

Example: A TV spot for Apple Computers introduces the world's smallest and largest laptops at 12 and 17 inches, respectively. The spot uses 7-foot-5 basketball phenom Yao Ming (Houston Rockets) and the 32-inch-tall actor Verne Troyer (best known for his role as Mini Me in the *Austin Powers* films). This spot playfully juxtaposes big and little, as it shows Verne with the 17-inch and Yao with the 12-inch computer, sitting side by side on an airplane.

Heavy/Light
Wide/Narrow
Thick/Thin

Also related to size are the key sensory metaphor of heavy/light and two related metaphors: wide/narrow and thick/thin. These three metaphors are similar in that they are ways of talking about density. Their central issue is whether the bulk supplied by being heavy, wide, or thick is beneficial or not.

Bulk can make the object or person look powerful and plush, but it can also make things look plodding and prosaic. On the flip side, to lack bulk by being light, narrow, or thin may enable speed and slick, sheer pleasure.

Example: A stylish felt hat that sits on the car's hood distinguishes a Buick print ad. The juxtaposition suggests casual elegance and establishes an effective contrast between the car's weighty presence and the sleek hat. The emotional pay dirt lies in the idea that the offer, the car, makes you fleet-footed and stylish.

In/Out (Inside/Outside)

To be in or on the inside resonates strongly with humans because it promises shelter and support. On an environmental basis, being in or inside implies protection from the elements. It's a secure place.

Socially, to be "in" means belonging. You're part of the group. You're "in the know," allowed to share knowledge and get allies. The social connection between "in" and intimacy or closeness reaches its physical and emotional peak in romance, when we say, "They're in love."

> *We tend to place great value on being in or inside something. We want to belong. It is the center, a place of nourishment, where the power is.*

Japanese and Spanish cultures are examples of drawing a clear distinction between the inside and the outside. For the Japanese, navigating a crowded world means that everything gets carefully compartmentalized. To be inside a group is vital; outsider status invites disdain. Meanwhile, for the Spanish, long besieged by foreign enemies, homes include gates, bars, and the sanctum of an inner courtyard.

To be on the periphery does typically mean being an outsider, a foreigner. To be out is often to lack resources, to be in danger, as indicated by idiomatic expressions like "out of the loop."

The exposure that comes with being on the outside can also be positive. Managers encourage their employees to "think outside the box," for example, because too much similarity is a threat to corporate survival.

To be on the outside can be exhilarating—liberation from confining conventions, restrictions, and obligations. But it often comes at the price of greater exertion.

Example: A Columbia Sportswear ad shows a red parka beneath the headline: "Hoods are all the rage on Paris runways. Like we give a crap." This is a great ad and an effective use of the in/out metaphor. The rugged, outdoorsy target audience for the offer will enjoy a joke that makes fun of the fashion world (which is obviously not the target for Columbia Sportswear).

Angular/Curved
Straight/Jagged
Vertical/Horizontal

These are all visual metaphors that communicate meaning through the arrangement of lines, shapes, and the basic geometric orientation on display.

For proof of the importance of some of these metaphors, consider the following example. Ronald Reagan's press secretary, Michael Deaver, prepared for the 1984 Republican convention by making sure that the podium and the other sights to be shown on TV within the convention hall consisted of round, soft features without any corners. He did this to offset what he feared was Reagan's unacceptable "warrior" image among some critical swing voters.

Deaver's concern that people's reactions to design elements invoke emotional responses and associations was right on target. For example, one cross-cultural study resulted in an 87 to 99 percent rate of agreement in an exercise that involved pairing visual elements to emotionally oriented adjectives.

Other common findings about angular versus round shapes that have emerged from research conducted around the world include the following:

- Although angles are considered to be hard, powerful, furious, serious, and full of agitation, curves, by comparison, are variously described as quiet, gentle, lazy, weak, playful, merry, or sad.

- In terms of direction, *upward* expressed qualities such as agitated, furious, powerful, playful, and merry. *Flat* was most commonly chosen to reflect qualities like quiet, gentle, serious, and hard. *Downward* was the most common choice for conveying that something was dead, lazy, weak, and sad.

- Linear forms that involved more angles and diagonals were considered to be more masculine and suggested activity, potency, and anger. Softer, round forms were thought of as more feminine and conveyed warmth, happiness, and goodness.

Interestingly enough, the correlation between angularity/anger versus round/happiness fits perfectly with facial coding. People in the studies related form to an emotional state.

In daily life people instinctively recognize the basic mood of others by whether the lines in their faces are more V-shaped or are instead rounder, softer, and more inviting. Such information is vital and hard-wired into us through evolution so that we know whether to avoid or approach. We want to know if we're in harm's way.

Observing a person who's frowning—whose face takes on a more angular shape—naturally makes us uneasy. We are on high-alert to pronounced angularity.

Example: In an ad for the recent James Bond movie *Die Another Day*, the camera follows the stars' hands as they move their guns in a sharp downward, counterclockwise angle. This motion conveys danger and power.

Damp/Dry
Relaxed/Tense

What unites these two sensory metaphors is that they're often about rejuvenation.

To be dry can mean safety, as in above the flood waters; but ultimately, as a species we must have access to water to survive. Therefore, dampness, as in moisture, is desirable. Moreover, it gives us energy, replenishment. When we discover water, we can relax, saving our energy.

By comparison, when we tense up, we expend energy. Tight muscles and higher blood pressure are two of nature's ways of getting one ready to face expected danger. These responses enable our bodies to help protect and promote our interests.

Example: Plenty of women's skin-care product ads have used water imagery to convey rejuvenation, youthfulness (as in dewy-soft skin), moisture, and freshness. An ad for Blistex lip balm shows a model soaked in the rain. This imagery is perhaps a bit overdone, but it speaks well to the need for hydration and replenishment.

More Universal Sensory Metaphors

The final group of metaphors are those with applications for two or more senses. There are two metaphors split evenly between sight and sound; two that work with sight, sound, and touch; and three more that tend to favor a visual application but can be relevant with the other senses as well.

High/Low (Up/Down)

In general, human preferences are for high (or up) over low (down).

There are many reasons for this bias. For one thing, to be higher up often provides more protection. From the top of a hill, we can survey the ground below and be more prepared to defend ourselves. This advantage may help explain the adage that "height is for men what beauty is for women"—in other words, a desirable trait.

It's not only true that taller people can see more; they can also exert more control. We speak in terms of being "on top of the situation" for a reason: To stand above or over an object enables a person to exert more power by pushing down on it while aided by gravity's force. Thus being "on top" or "above" translates to a sense of superiority.

There are two additional reasons for the general bias in favor of high (or up). The first is that up can mean more; think of how we talk of how the stock market is "rising" or "falling." Quantity and verticality are intimately associated in our minds through experiences of the material world.

The second is that to be up is to be happy, as in "I'm feeling up today."

> To be up is to be energetic, to soar, to be free. Older people shrink in stature, whereas youth is looking to peak.

Although feeling low is linked to dissatisfaction, being low (down) can also be good at times. Yes, life as a bottom-dweller isn't much good, but at the same time, clichés like having "both feet on the ground" or being "down to earth" indicate the value of staying in touch, exhibiting humility, and generally not exposing oneself to harm by getting too arrogant or "uppity."

Example: A solid, appropriate use of the high/low metaphor is a Fidelity Investments ad. It shows a gray-haired man sitting with a woman (presumably his daughter) on a veranda looking down on a bay. The estate's manicured grounds, the vista, and the goal of retiring "with the most money" combine to link quality, height, and quantity.

Fast/Slow

The sensory metaphor of motion, as in speed, is central to not only our lifestyle as a society but also the efficiency of the offers that companies are providing. It isn't by chance that Microsoft's tagline refers to motion: "Where do you want to go today?"

We have lots of experiential associations to fit the concept of motion, associations that probably start with learning to walk as a child.

Motion is progress, and the ability to go fast is generally more valued than going slow. People tend to equate being fast both with being smart and increasing productivity or general level of achievement.

In contrast, going slow raises concerns that progress is being blocked, diverted, or otherwise thwarted. Despite the fable about the tortoise and the hare, being slow is rarely considered a virtue except in industries like banking and insurance, in which prudence is welcome by consumers.

Example: An exception that favors slowness is an ad for NYK Cruises that made the concept of "Life in motion" its tagline. The visual shows a luxury cruise liner moving slowly across a bay. Here, going slow is an appreciated quality. The heart of this offer's promise is peacefulness and relaxation, including a quiet ride and open space.

Full/Open
Tight/Loose

These two metaphors share the issue of whether greater density (full and tight) is a virtue that signals more depth or if it should be equated with overwhelming, restrictive mass. The sound of a full orchestra, for instance, can be vibrant or unappealingly thunderous, depending on how it strikes us. Likewise, *open* and *loose* are fairly ambiguous. They can mean free and easy, but they can also indicate sparseness and a lack of substance or structure.

In psychological terms, what underlies the metaphors of full/open and tight/loose is akin to wanting the optimal degree of personal space. To experience something that's full or tight

*can make us feel like we're under pressure, buried, and
trapped. As a species, humans value having enough room to
maneuver. To be in close quarters with something isn't comfortable and can readily translate into danger.*

On the other hand, extreme openness or looseness can—like
excessive distance between two talking people—make one feel too
disconnected. We instinctively sense a gap or void separating us.
The happy medium is finding things that fit well, forming a snug,
unifying relationship.

Example: A Breyers ice cream ad reinforces its message of fewer
calories with a clean, simple layout on an all-white background. Depicted alongside the headline, "Less fat, few calories, no guilt," are
three cartons of ice cream in a small enough size that the take-away
impression is that of openness—thereby reinforcing the notion that
this treat won't fill you up so much that your pants feel tight.

Chaotic/Orderly

This sensory metaphor is related to dirty/clean while also taking
on design issues like uniformity, variety, balance, repetition, and
symmetry.

*People are biased in favor of the orderly. Consumers look for a
pattern. The reason patterns are so important is because we're
hard-wired through evolution to classify stimuli. This process
enables a person to understand and react to circumstances with
more speed and ease, which is clearly an adaptive advantage.*

Example: A print ad for the organizing system California Closets shows a sun-filled bedroom with an impeccable closet in the

background. This idea of having an organized closet is appealing because many neglect their closets and seeing this space in perfect order hints that this closet owner has everything in his or her life under control—even the closets are perfect.

Hard/Soft (Strong/Weak)

Of all the sensory metaphors, this one most easily fits the standard, stereotypical gender gap dichotomy between male and female associations. To be hard and strong is to be masculine (typically), with all the obvious gender overtones. The inverse is, of course, the old equation of feminine with softness and, generally speaking, less physical strength.

Today, women's greater participation in competitive enterprises like business and sports has begun to blur this distinction, but regardless of gender, the sensory-emotive concept of somebody or something being either as "tough as nails" or else sensitive and "soft" lives on.

Example: A Tylenol ad featuring arthritis pain seizes on this metaphor and invokes both ends of the spectrum between hard and soft. The ad shows a woman with her leg raised on a chair while she fastens the buckle of her high-heeled shoes. Her body has been soft, we assume. But with the help of the product's "strength," she's more limber and able to "fight back" so that she can enjoy an active social life again.

New/Old
Simple/Complex

Finally, there is one crucial pair of sensory metaphors worth considering before this chapter concludes. It's crucial because what unites new/old with simple/complex is that together they help determine the degree to which any marketing effort will break through the clutter and appeal to the buying public.

In short, these metaphors, which apply to all of the senses, get to the heart of perception—which is the issue of clarity. The split between new versus old can also be thought of as the distinction between novelty and familiarity. Both of those qualities have their own strengths and weaknesses, but most people are receptive to the right mixture of interest and ease.

Novelty can provoke interest. Anything unusual and surprising—in a word, rare—will tend to draw our senses. But the problem is that it may not *hold* the senses and may also fail to draw the heart enough to induce an emotional engagement.

Something that is novel may initially capture attention, but it runs the risk of not playing to what the mind–body already knows. Consumers want the familiar. That's the issue—a chance to bring past associations to bear on something new.

Research suggests that what works best along the new/old spectrum is a modest mismatch between what we know—and expect—and something fresh and interesting.

To emphasize novelty beyond the respect shown for the familiar doesn't work very well. The reason why the mind categorizes things is to economize its energies. As a result, humans are constantly looking to diagnose how well the new stimulus fits the characteristics of the category assigned to it.

The simple/complex metaphor also involves interest, ease, and overall clarity, but compared to the new/old metaphor, the split is between simplicity as basic and familiar and complexity as more sophisticated and novel. In this case, what's complex may provide the interest. Consumer senses are also attracted by a fair amount of information because they are receptive to investigating possibilities. In doing so, people are trying to establish relevancy and determine whether the stimulus may enhance life or become threatening. Consumers are modestly willing to learn about what's useful to them.

As research shows, complexity has the merit of offering information from which to learn. The result is that over repeated exposure, a complex stimulus can hold its own because it gives viewers the chance to keep hunting for helpful, life-enhancing data.

At the same time, however, a complex stimulus has great vulnerability at the front end of the perception process. It doesn't provide enough ease. It's the equivalent of a nine-digit ZIP code that we never quite memorize.

In the end, what's simple is easy but runs the risk of inducing boredom over the long haul.

Any stimulus should be simple enough to engage a person initially—through its clarity—but not be so basic and familiar that consumers soon lose the ability to be intrigued by it.

Example: The Hartford Financial Services Group made an insurance ad that took the familiar and, by isolating it, gave it the force of novelty (see Figure 7.1). The visual is the palm of a hand and two different points along a wrinkle in the palm. The simple, effective headline reads: "Would you like to retire here? Or here?"

Now that I've covered the key sensory metaphors by which consumers consciously or unconsciously organize responses to the world, the sensory part of sensory-emotive offer positioning is in place. Next up is an explanation of how and why key emotions function the way they do, including perspective on what business can do to better leverage the ways that consumers' feelings unfold.

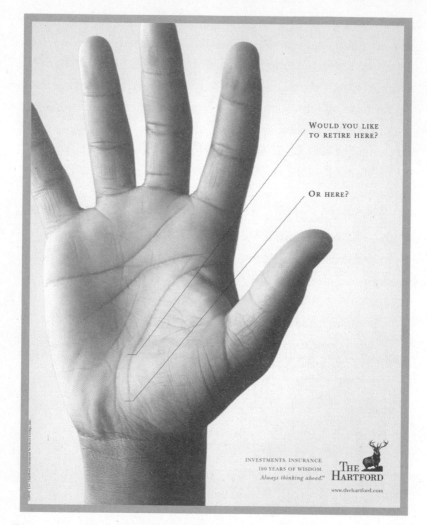

Figure 7.1 This Hartford Financial Services Group ad uses the new/old, simple/complex dynamics in a striking way. What's more commonplace than the human hand? The successful ad relies on clever copy that integrates concept (retirement options) and visual imagery seamlessly. The hand, simply photographed against a white background, renders the familiar visually complex and fascinating. (Reprinted with permission from The Hartford Financial Services Group, Inc.)

Using Emotive Scripts

Tapping into Consumers' Emotional Memory Banks

In Chapter 2, I explained why people are emotional decision makers. Now I will describe how you can use that natural orientation on behalf of your company's brand marketing efforts.

What is an emotive script? Let's build the definition in a two-step process, beginning with the concept of a script. As Roger Shank says, "A script is a set of expectations about what will happen next in a well-understood situation. Life experience means quite often knowing how to act and how others will act in a given stereotypical situation. That knowledge is called a script."[1] For example, when you see a friend on the street, you'll probably ask, "How are you?" Perhaps you end a conversation by saying, "Have a good day." These are both scripts that people follow all the time in interactions with others.

Consumers have scripts, too, as I'll explain. To know what consumers will do—and why—obviously provides a strategic business advantage, which is the reason the goal of exploring scripts is so valuable to companies. Because humans are primarily emotional decision makers, the single most crucial set of scripts a company wants to have at its disposal are the emotive scripts that drive consumers and determine market share.

Fortunately, emotive scripts are feasible to construct. The truth is that there are different action tendencies for the core emotions that facial coding helps address. Moreover, evolutionary psychology lends a hand by relating emotions to human nature and basic needs, thereby supporting the conclusion that "many emotion scripts are not idiosyncratic."[2]

In essence, every emotion has a logic of its own. There are ways that a core emotion physically manifests itself, and there are causes, behaviors, and themes that pertain to each of these emotions.

The causes are occasionally purely memory-induced; even then, the memory typically takes the form of a visual or auditory image. Most of the time they are the result of sensory clues within the immediate environment. Those clues trigger a quick, often largely unconscious emotional reaction, which in turn leads to an outcome whose action involves both the body and mind.

As for the themes of these emotions, they generally involve such basic aspirations and dilemmas as being loved or rejected, gaining power or being powerless, and proving to be either triumphant or victimized. More specifically, they reflect a given emotion's story line— what is revealed about a consumer's relation to experiencing a company's offer or interfacing with its employees in a service situation.

Once these emotive scripts have been triggered and set into motion, they are fixed. Therefore, what a company needs to do is be aware of those scripts, position the offer and marketing in relation to them, enhance any positive outcome, and mitigate (whenever possible) any negative outcome.

The Major Emotive Scripts

If a brand is to have real staying power, it must interact with the consumer at the gut level, and it needs to generate emotional resonance. Therefore, the emotive script—the story—of how the branded offer *feels* to the consumer is highly relevant to generating sales.

> Ask yourself: What story are you inviting potential customers into? What emotions get activated, and how can you be sure they will connect consumers to your brand in a positive way?

Those are questions marketers must ask themselves. In doing so, they must understand the emotional architecture of how feelings are structured because the major emotive scripts need to be well managed. In what follows, I focus on the seven core emotions that facial coding expert Paul Ekman has identified as commonly evident across cultures.[3] In addition, I include an emotion of my own choosing—pride, an emotion that's really a robust version of reassurance because it so often motivates consumer purchase behavior.

Positive Emotions

It's sad to say, but there are only two positive feelings common and essential enough to business to be worth addressing here: One is *happiness*, which ranges from ecstasy and joy to serenity and calmness. Love, lust, optimism, and contentment are all related terms that also live in the general neighborhood of happiness. The other feeling is *pride* (reassurance), which bears relation to admiration, esteem, respect, satisfaction, encouragement, acceptance, and comfort.

Happiness

The pursuit of happiness is described in the Declaration of Independence as American citizens' inalienable right. Of course, every brand marketer strives to instill this feeling in consumers. It should come as no surprise then that a survey of American TV advertising found some sort of happiness or having fun depicted in 57 percent of the ads and in over 80 percent of those promoting soft drinks, children's toys, and restaurants.

Everyone probably thinks they know happiness when they experience it. But exactly what *is* it?

- *Dynamics of happiness.* Happiness is a feeling we can usually see coming over the horizon. We ease into it.

Happiness is often the result of social relationships and involves love, liking, affection, and general acceptance—factors one may anticipate but doesn't have much control over.

- *Physical manifestations.* Physically, this emotion creates a warm body temperature, an accelerated heartbeat, smiles, and, in strong cases, laughter. In response to this feeling, people tend to have

(continued)

open body language, be outgoing, and seek contact. People will willingly and enthusiastically approach the source of happiness and welcome its approach in return. This emotion's basic orientation involves connectedness—we want to court, gain, possess, and be possessed.

- *Themes of happiness.* Consumers are often pleased about an event or circumstance related to their well-being. We've experienced gain or success and have made or are now making reasonable progress toward a goal. The world seems just, open, benevolent—a place of enjoyment. Often, this feeling has either an explicit or implicit sexual nature to it, involving mating or otherwise being both open and sharing. Though often communal in orientation, the human hope for happiness encompasses a variety of motivations, including desire for success, pleasure, abundance, stability, health, and well-being.

Example: Volkswagen's New Beetle ads epitomize a feeling of happiness, playing off the friendly, fuss-free design of the products themselves and capturing the feel-good spirit of the 1960s that the cars have long represented. Set against a simple, bright white background, these straightforward ads feature tongue-in-cheek headlines such as, "0 to 60? Yes." These ads remind us why the cars are singular, evoking feelings of happy nostalgia.

Pride/Reassurance

Among the emotions discussed, this is the only one for which there isn't a facial coding diagnosis. This feeling is really in many ways less of a biological imperative—it's less of a feeling that helps a person adapt as it is an ego/social feeling. Pride and reassurance are more a matter of feeling good about ourselves in an egocentric manner, and only secondarily a matter of attracting allies or envy by exuding such confidence.

In business, pride (the strongest version of reassurance) can be of vital strategic benefit. Because comfort and security are essential concerns of people, a branded offer that can instill reassurance—all the way to pride—enjoys a tremendous advantage.

- *Dynamics of pride.* Like happiness, this is an emotion people often see coming over the horizon. It's likely to fit one's expectations or at least one's hopes. This feeling can involve gaining the gratitude or admiration of others, but pride is basically a self-caused emotion.

  We're approving of our own actions. Pride confirms the value of a self-initiated act that we (and perhaps others) deem praiseworthy.

- *Physical manifestations.* Again, we're unable to detect pride from facial coding, but it's a very comforting emotion. Its counterpart, reassurance, is oriented to behavior that involves incorporation,

  (continued)

affiliation, bonding, and generally manifesting trust. In an underlying sense, pride and reassurance are about receiving and accepting ourselves and our own decisions based on the support of external stimuli.

- *Themes of pride.* Pride concerns the enhancement of one's identity or sense of self-worth by taking credit for a valued object or achievement. The object or achievement is likely to be our own, but it could also involve others with whom we identify. If a single word embodies this feeling it's *respect*—we feel better about ourselves. In comparison to pride, the feeling of reassurance involves a dynamic based more on gaining confidence by restoring (rather than enhancing) it. To be reassured typically means that a fear or risk has been removed. We're safe, sure, certain—we've realized attainment or a better condition. We're beyond reproach, approved of, even eligible for praise.

Example: A Kodak ad has the headline "Pride. Magnified times ten," and makes proper use of this emotion. The original photograph up in a corner shows a girl alongside two other track stars, each of them hugging a trophy. The larger, main photograph is a cropped, close-up enhancement of one girl being showcased for her accomplishment. Because pride involves individual growth, the fact that Kodak's Picture Maker technology literally increased the size of the girl's photo suitably links the emotion and the offer.

Negative Emotions

Among the core emotions that facial coding addresses, negative feelings predominate. That's not surprising when one considers that it's the human survival instinct that causes a person to hear bad news first and loudest. Two of the four core negative emotions are active (anger and disgust) and two are more passive in nature (sadness and fear).

Anger

Anger is the negative emotion that companies most clearly want to avoid creating in their customers or in consumers at large. Among other causes, anger can be the result of offensive advertising, of advertising that gets itself into trouble by overpromising what the offer can deliver, or of bad customer service. Misunderstanding this emotion will only make it harder to handle on those occasions when it does arise.

There is some potential upside to anger, however. Like the other emotions, to cause a consumer to make an emotional decision provides a means of getting out of the commodity trap because price becomes either a smaller or nonexistent factor. Therefore, anger or resentment can be used for cause-related marketing that may involve issues as diverse as "buying American" or only alternative, "green" products. As with humor, anger used well can work great. But when it fails, it misses by a mile.

> • *Dynamics of anger.* Unlike happiness, anger is a feeling that often catches people by surprise. It's highly relevant to goals that are being interfered
>
> *(continued)*

with or obstructed. It can be caused by an object, but anger often begins in reaction to the communication or actions of other people. Insults, criticism, and rejection can result in this emotion, as can the omission or termination of a reward.

If anything sums up the cause of anger, it's violated expectations.

- *Physical manifestations.* Heart rate accelerates, muscles tense up, temperature rises, and people generally heat up and get energized to fight whatever is felt to be an obstacle. When angry, people tend to move toward—against—people or objects because they are on the attack to overcome the problem.

- *Themes of anger.* It's not just that there seems to be a barrier to progress, it's that the barrier is believed to be unfair. A sense of injustice and anger often go hand in hand. People find the interference or the harm to be illegitimate, even demeaning. The offense that made us angry may be characterized as aggressive, incompetent, or threatening to a relationship. Deep down, we often interpret assaults that make us angry as an attack on our personal identity, our sense of self-worth. We're sure we're right. So we dislike or even despise the source of our distress.

Anger is a reactionary response—a lashing out. It's the *fight* part of our fight-or-flight instinct as we seek to gain respect.

Example: An ad for Ragú's meat sauce shows three frowning butchers, two of them with their arms crossed, and the headline: "We asked these butchers what they thought of our new meat sauce. They beat us up." I don't think this is the best use of anger—for example, the chefs bear no relation to a consumer's point of view—but anger can be difficult to depict. In this case, Ragu is clearly trying to use anger to be funny.

Disgust (Contempt)

Whereas anger is about feeling rejected, cheated, mishandled, and shown disrespect, disgust is about deliberately or involuntarily rejecting something or someone.

> *Disgust and its related emotion, contempt, are also the inverse of pride and reassurance. Instead of seeking affiliation, establishing distance or a gap between yourself and the unwanted stimulus becomes the goal.*

Disgust (or contempt) for a product is clearly the antithesis of desired consumer behavior. This feeling stands in the way of promoting brand loyalty. Unfortunately for the business world, a milder form of disgust—boredom—is common in response to marketing efforts that don't foresee the sensory-emotive reaction they will trigger.

> • *Dynamics of disgust.* Disgust and contempt are similar in that they result from a negative, *aver-*
> (continued)

sive reaction. There are several subtle differences between these two emotions, however, because disgust is more unexpected, can be in response to either objects or people, and involves more urgency (and therefore less control).

- *Physical manifestations.* In physical terms, both feelings make people tense as they repulse something or someone with behavior that involves moving away, pushing away, rejection, expulsion, and, at times, even vomiting. If there's a single operative word here it's *poison.* We find what we've encountered to be toxic, and naturally the response is to expel it from perhaps our body and certainly from our list of preferences.

- *Themes of disgust.* With both disgust and contempt, we feel as though we've been too intimate—too accepting—of an object, idea, person, or other harmful stimuli that is, in the end, either indigestible or better off avoided entirely. Underneath it all, what these two emotions are really about is a fear of falling subject to disease and illness. The adaptive advantage of disgust lies in getting rid of something that we have previously incorporated into our lives. Loathing, repulsion, and rejection are the operative terms that reflect a spirit of good riddance as we blame, find fault, and generally become hostile to whatever it is that provoked us.

Example: A Tilex mildew remover ad dramatizes this emotion for all it's worth. The visual is a grainy photograph showing men lathered up in a shower. The headline reads, "One coal mine, 22 showers and the everyday grime of 622 sooty men." The offer's promise of killing mildew is evidence of the powerful, biological impulse (disgust) that this emotion involves.

Sadness

Sadness can prove to be an important emotion in business because of buyer's regret. The result of such remorse is that consumers are inevitably not inclined to repeat the purchase, thereby injuring if not destroying the prospects for a long-term brand-customer relationship.

Buyer's regret can happen for a variety of reasons, including a poor-quality product, inferior customer service, or bait-and-switch advertising practices. As a purchase becomes less important to a person, regret can lead one to sever the relationship altogether.

> * *Dynamics of sadness.* Sadness is a feeling people can't really control and don't readily expect to have happen. Sadness can be caused by either a person or an object but tends to be based primarily in social interaction. Common causes include suffering rejection and general social isolation. This emotion can also be caused by the omission or termination of a reward. In short, sadness is due to a threat that has already been realized.
>
> *(continued)*

- *Physical manifestations*. The physical reaction is to undergo a drop in body temperature, which corresponds to avoidance behavior. People withdraw, become listless, and grieve. Often, we literally cry to be reunited with what we lost and needed or enjoyed. Although we might cry for help or seek a replacement, giving up is the most typical response.

- *Themes of sadness*. A sad person feels as if he or she has experienced an irrevocable loss. At times, of course, sadness does stem from a loss, but regardless of the actual source, this sensation often results in a flat mood and feelings of helplessness. As with anger, a person feels as though a goal has been thwarted or otherwise obstructed, but there are important differences between these two feelings. With sadness, the notion of justice is usually irrelevant. Unlike anger, which results in getting energized, when we're sad, we slow down, as if to protect ourselves from getting into any additional danger. We want to reunite with what we got separated from, reintegrating and, thereby, nurturing ourselves.

Example: An ad for Olay's Total Effects Visible Anti-Aging Vitamin Complex shows a slightly melancholy woman photographed in black and white. The loss or separation involved here is a matter of moving away from youth. The use of sadness is appropriate, but whether the ad is effective depends on if the scientifically oriented copy convinces women that this offer can really reduce distress by being able to fight seven signs of aging, as it claims.

Fear

The marketplace is full of flight. In its mildest form, consumers often don't feel like they have the time, energy, or conviction to consider an offer. They will pass by, moving away from it. At a more intense level, this kind of flight can reflect a full-blown fear that the offer is hype and, in buying it, one will look stupid in addition to being taken advantage of.

> *As a species, humans share a natural, instinctive concern for safety, protection, and the prevention of harm to ourselves. Whether an offer is safe is the first check point on our mental list—the equivalent of looking both ways before crossing the street. When developing an effective marketing strategy, it's imperative to ensure that the offer will not induce feelings of fear and related emotions like doubt, worry, anxiety, and embarrassment.*

Fear comes in many forms within the business arena. There's the negative fear of being vulnerable by allowing oneself to be tricked by a bogus operation, as well as the motivating fear of missing a deal if one doesn't respond to a limited-time offer. Either way, fear cuts through the clutter like little else.

- *Dynamics of fear.* Fear is a feeling that usually happens unexpectedly and has its roots in social rejection, failure, loss, or a concern about a future

(continued)

difficulty. It is also entirely possible that fear may stem from immediate, specific physical danger or pain.

- *Physical manifestations.* When people are afraid, heart rate rises, muscles tense, and body temperature cools as they go into a cold sweat. In terms of body language, when responding to fear, we tend to make ourselves into as small a target as we can. Fear is clearly the *flight* part of fight-or-flight. We seek to escape a perceived danger to protect ourselves and not get destroyed. Literal, physical flight (fleeing) is possible. But so is mental suppression of the threat as a more passive means of calming ourselves down.

- *Themes of fear.* The crucial psychological basis of this feeling is that one might feel helpless. We're without power and up against a source of threat or danger that we dislike but can't do much about. Fear can seem like a punishment. It's as if the world is being malevolent—offering only undesirable outcomes. Part of what makes fear so powerful is that people often feel like they're trying to protect themselves against a force of unknown dimension and duration.

Example: A Swiss Life (investments and insurance) ad promotes its employee benefit plans by showing a young man who is naked from the waist up and photographed in blue light. The promise of security, a respite from fear, is represented by a pool of water in his cupped hands and the headline, "Don't let your resources drain away. Pool them." The power of the ad in terms of portraying fear is that it implies a dramatic threat to our environment or our resources, suggesting that we must conserve our own resources and not let them slip away (the way the water will easily drain from his hands). In showing a half-naked man with the photo tinged in blue, this ad also relates to the physical manifestation of fear—losing body heat—and speaks to a sense of vulnerability that comes in being naked.

A Neutral Emotion

Surprise, to some psychologists, is arguably not even an emotion but a sort of pre-emotion. According to that line of analysis, surprise transforms itself into some other, negative or positive (emotional) response after a person has finished a quick appraisal of the new stimulus. Most psychologists, however, consider it to be a valid emotion in its own right; for marketing purposes, surprise is often an essential ingredient to achieve success.

Surprise

> *This emotion relates to novelty and the chance to cut through the clutter and create excitement. Surprise draws attention to an offer. It can be very appropriate if the offer is new or has new features, applications, or ways of being promoted.*

As a species, humans tend to be afraid of what's new (e.g., a sneak attack). Therefore, people are cautious. We don't want to be embarrassed by making a wrong decision, so tried-and-true strategies can work better. But at the same time, there are good surprises, such as surprise parties and the delight of Christmas gifts. Therefore, surprise is seen as a mixed blessing, and that's where the creative tension resides—in mining the potential of surprise while trying to avoid bringing to mind the notion of risk.

- *Dynamics of surprise*. Surprise is, by definition, a feeling that we don't expect to have. Therefore, the potential for controlling surprise is virtually nonexistent. This emotion can be either positive or negative and be caused by a stimulus that isn't so original as it is unexpected in terms of timing or the place where we experience it.

- *Physical manifestations*. Surprise is a very protective emotion. The model is that a person stops, freezes, and tries to get oriented to the new, unexpected stimulus. The question we essentially ask ourselves is, "What is it?" The advantage of this feeling is that it readies us for action when we have encountered a strange, unevaluated item. We're protecting ourselves by suspending action in the face of novelty until we can understand the change.

- *Themes of surprise*. This emotion is really about being struck by the unexpected. This blow may be physical or psychological, but its effect results in a complete mind/body reaction. In a word, we are trying to regain our *equilibrium*. While doing so, the instinct is to freeze or, in effect, close our-

(continued)

selves off from the new stimulus as a protective measure. The disorienting state associated with this feeling makes being taken unawares the equivalent of going numb. Surprise relates to curiosity because both involve trying to solve a mystery through scrutiny. The difference is that curiosity often involves less of a surprise due to more self-directed inquiry.

Example: A Secret deodorant ad equates surprise with nervousness. The ad shows two young couples in a kitchen, presumably about to have dinner—except that the hostess has opened the oven door only to be met by smoke. To the extent that the hostess's specialty dish may now be a culinary disaster, surprise is the emotion that fits the moment even if the creative execution isn't very surprising. Surprise heightens the need for a product that protects consumers from the additional strain of social embarrassment brought on by the noticeable odor or visible wetness of becoming nervous.

Appealing to universal emotive scripts can be a powerful way to get consumers' attention. In the next chapter, I'll discuss other implications of evolutionary psychology for marketers, revealing more tactics for appealing to all consumers across age, gender, and cultural lines.

Notes

1. Roger Shank, *Tell Me a Story: A New Look at Real and Artificial Memory* (New York: Charles Scribner's Sons, 1990), 6.

2. Ibid., 7.

3. Books by Ekman include *Telling Lies: Clues to Deceit in the Marketplace, Politics and Marriage* (New York: Norton, 1985); with Richard J. Davidson, *The Nature of Emotion* (New York: Oxford University Press, 1994); with Erika L. Rosenberg, eds., *What the Face Reveals: Basic and Applied Studies of Spontaneous Expression Using the Facial Action Coding System (FACS)* (New York: Oxford University Press USA, 1998).

Consumers' Evolutionary Needs

Appealing to Humans' Innate Desires

Among the elements required to create deeper, sensory-emotive offer positioning, two of the three sets of variables have now been introduced: the key sensory metaphors, and a group of essential emotions. The set that awaits an introduction is *needs*, notably the basic human needs that evolutionary psychology addresses.

First I'll answer the following question: What exactly is evolutionary psychology, and why does it matter to the business world?

Evolutionary psychology combines diverse academic fields like cognitive science, evolutionary biology, genetics, and neuropsychology. I will take that explanation a step further by noting that evolutionary psychologists seek to explore and understand the basic human condition. It's a field that has been called modern Darwinism. The label fits because evolutionary psychology pursues Darwin's focus on the fundamental ways in which human beings struggle to improve the odds of survival.

Here's a summary of the evolutionary psychology's main concepts.

There are aspects of human behavior that are fairly inherent and universal. These motivational tendencies have been hard-wired into humans over the course of evolution because they have been proven necessary or helpful for the species to thrive.

More specifically, behaviors that we tend to practice in an effort to secure resources and protect our interests include:

- Granting primacy to family ties;

- Driving toward dominance;

- Exhibiting a bias toward sharing based on reciprocity (in other words, scientific confirmation of why the what's-in-it-for-me approach is so important).

The sensory information (clues) most relevant to survival involves behavioral options. Humans search the environment to identify what is useful, helpful, and potentially harmful.

None of those concepts may, in themselves, seem likely to spark controversy. But as scholars like Edward O. Wilson (*Sociobiology*) and Steven Pinker (*The Blank Slate*) know full well, the related idea that human nature may be sharply influenced if not largely driven by biology and, specifically, genetic makeup is a very sensitive issue.[1]

I don't intend to advocate the notion that every human being is identical. Clearly, cultural differences, peer groups, and experiences play a significant role in how we become who we are. But I also don't believe the business world should or can afford to steer clear of investigating the motivations that define human nature. A brand marketing program that doesn't use the insights of brain scientists—like those of behavioral economists and evolutionary psychologists—really isn't going to be as successful as it could be.

Part of what these scientists have been discovering pertains to matters like emotional decision making and the role of the amygdala and hippocampus. But at other times this research also appears to support innate behavioral differences between the two genders that involve more than just reproductive functions.

It isn't the purpose of this volume—a business book—to resolve such gigantic issues as nature versus nurture or the profound differences between men and women. However, by introducing needs (from a gender perspective), I aim to outline the basic needs that evolutionary psychology dwells on. The marketing advantage of doing so is that given the importance of the mind–body link, the most basic force that creates segmentation—biological differences based on gender—must also be addressed to make the positioning process complete and accurate. Furthermore, with this last variable in place—gendered needs—you'll then be ready to develop a sensory-emotive positioning to the necessary degree.

Basic Human Needs

Identifying and understanding basic human needs is vital to business. Only by touching base with—and leveraging—the core motives that drive behavior can a company make sure its offer is

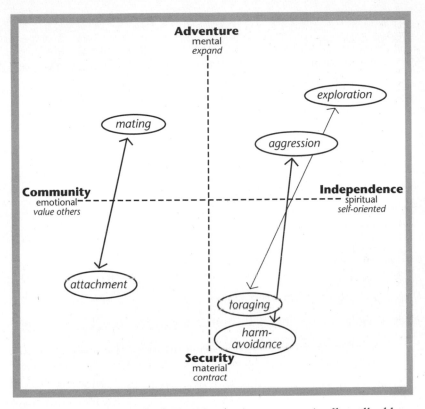

Figure 9.1 Orientation Grid: Key Needs. Any company's offer will address one or more of these inner needs that have been identified by evolutionary psychologists. For strategic purposes, the needs can also be evaluated in regard to consumers' basic orientations.

positioned strongly and deep enough to gain traction among consumers in the marketplace.

Certainly, not everyone involved in evolutionary psychology has exactly the same list or uses the same terminology to define these basic needs. However, enough of a consensus exists that it's feasible to focus on six specific needs worth discussing. As shown by the accompanying chart (see Figure 9.1), these needs also correspond pretty well with six key emotional markets that Rolf Jensen elaborates on in *The Dream Society*.[2]

Search Needs

The category that I'm calling search needs consists of foraging and exploration. What these needs have in common is an instinct for acquiring. People scour their surroundings to secure resources that will fulfill either physical or more intellectual requirements for nourishment.

Foraging

The search for food and drink to stay alive is as basic as it gets. In relation to Maslow's hierarchy of needs, the need to forage matches the lowest, most basic rung on his ladder—and includes such basic physical needs as getting enough air and sleep.

Back in the hunter-gatherer stage of human existence, our ancestors had to forage on an almost daily basis to meet their nutritional needs. This may partly account for why humans like lakes and rivers so much. They quench not only our thirst but also the thirst of other animals. A body of water has therefore always been likely to signal the presence of game for hunting as a means of putting food on the table.

Among other evidence, ancient cave paintings suggest that men were typically the hunters and the women the gatherers. A rudimentary division of labor might have made perfect sense back then, given the usually greater physical strength of men (of use in tracking wild animals). Meanwhile, the women found fruit and vegetables, handled the child rearing, and tended the home fires.

Today, much has changed. Dual-income households are common. More women are living alone and supporting themselves, and foraging has expanded as an activity to include not just food and drink but other necessities, as well as shopping for fun.

> As gatherers par excellence, it has been estimated that women still buy or at least influence most of the shopping, including as much as 80 percent of all consumer goods purchases. As for what kind of shoppers they are, women are more careful than men, as Paco Underhill argues based on his years of studying consumer behavior in retail settings.[3] The men tend to be on hunt-and-kill missions. They enter the store, find what they want, and head out the door. The women seek an overview of available options, then weigh the advantages of one brand over another in determining which offer best meets their sensory-emotive as well as rational needs. Along with taking more time, women also take more pride in proving their ability to be discriminating shoppers who "feather the nest" well.

Example: A KitchenAid print ad for its kitchen products has as the largest visual the deliverable: a chocolate dessert. (Substitute barbecue for brownie and this ad would appeal to hunters rather than gatherers.) The copy ends with: "Bask in the glow of appreciative guests."

Eating a treat is hardly a basic need. But the link between good food, the home, and proving one's worth through the ability to generate oohs and aahs reveals the enduring power of foraging as central to the species' existence.

Exploration

Exploration is related to foraging, but it's not as functional. Exploration tends to be driven more by instinctive curiosity. Although foraging fits with the lowest rung on Maslow's hierarchy, exploration may come closest to matching the highest rung: the quest for self-actualization. Humans explore to fulfill potential.

Meanwhile, among Jensen's six emotional markets the best correspondence would appear to be between exploration and what he calls the adventure market. In business terms, the offers involved are diverse. They include travel, sports, video games, cars, movies, and books. The similarity among these things is that in every case, the item carries us beyond ourselves into a new experience.

Though discussed in relation to the sensory metaphors of simple/complex and new/old, the concepts of interest and ease apply to exploration as well. Something too simple and familiar can fail to arouse curiosity. Something too complicated and totally novel can, on the other hand, inhibit exploration.

Beyond those universal guidelines, however, possible gender differences emerge in regard to this need. For men, exploration is frequently *outward* in orientation. Men are linear, stepwise thinkers. Exploration is often a chance for men to separate themselves from others. Men distinguish themselves from others by developing strengths and demonstrating skills in challenging situations. Involvement with cars, video games, and sports are manifestations of that urge. At the same time, exploration can also be a team sport, as shown by adventure travel packages.

From my own readings and observations, as well as from talking to women about basic human needs, I have come to the conclusion that for women exploration can go either way—it can be directed outward or it can be inward in orientation. It seems to be more likely to be inward for women than for men. For instance, women are the vast majority of book buyers (and presumably readers) for most genres.

Why might this be true? Maybe it's because women are still often defined in terms of helping others. Women are the designated caretakers, brought up to be responsible for the well-being of those around them. Exploration represents an opportunity to nurture and replenish themselves, so to do something like visiting a spa provides a brief indulgence, a little self-pampering to offset all the energy given away.

These dual approaches to exploration are in keeping with research indicating that men are typically better at visual and spatial reasoning. In contrast, women's other, nonvisual senses are almost always much sharper in terms of picking up the subtle impact of smells, sounds, tastes, and tactile impressions.

Example: A Pioneer Electronics ad shows a young couple sitting on a couch. The man has the remote in his hand and is watching the TV with rapt attention while the woman has her head back, eyes fixed on the ceiling. The headline says, "The home theater system that's easier to figure out than your girlfriend."

This ad isn't particularly original. However, it confirms the dichotomy that so often exists between a technology-fixed male who identifies exploration on an outward basis, and a female who would likely prefer to be with someone willing and able to talk and, thus, explore on an inward basis what they might have to share.

Status Needs

The category that I'm calling status needs consists of aggression and harm avoidance. What they have in common is navigating the dynamics of power. Aggression relates to seeking dominance—over people, objects, or even a circumstance. Harm avoidance is the opposite. This need is about trying not to get physically or emotionally hurt by a more powerful, dominant force.

Aggression

Human beings are driven to achieve power. Truth be told, we're an aggressive species. Our history is marked by warfare, violence, and conquest. It's not a pretty picture, but the reality is that conflict and destruction are a big part of history on both national and personal levels.

Aggression can be loud, but it can also take a more quiet, subtle form on a daily basis. For instance, there are countless contests held to determine winners and losers. These and other challenges measure a person's degree of influence and relative strength, and these rituals and displays are meant to impress others.

The reason for all of this aggression seems to be a human need to establish status differentiation. We long to be perceived as powerful. If we don't achieve it, our tendency is to adopt a herding instinct and imitate those in power.

In regard to Maslow's hierarchy of needs, aggression most closely resembles the rung second to the top. For Maslow, esteem is about the human need to feel important and achieve self-respect, attention, and recognition.

As to Jensen's six emotional markets, aggression fits best with the market for the display of our beliefs. One example is cause-related behavior (like buying only organically grown produce) to challenge the status quo.

> Men often seek to establish dominance quite overtly.
> Their aggression takes the form of staking out their
>
> *(continued)*

> territory or otherwise showing off. They take action by making very conspicuous purchases—sports cars, big homes, fancy watches, and so on—that signal power.

The explanation for this behavior is partly related to testosterone. A second likely reason is that men typically have to be confident risk-takers and prove their providing ability to land a mate.

> What form does aggression take among women? Women like to show off, too, but their displays are less about being a powerful individual than about being well connected, well positioned, and in the know. In this case, words often get substituted for the actions men would resort to for wielding power. Women might discuss fashion, and who's "in" or "out." It's more relational, a game of gossip and negotiating the pecking order.

Example: A Best Buy ad for DVD movies features an "average Joe" consumer holding a *Rocky* DVD collection. Standing in front of a row of big-screen TVs that all show a close-up of the angry face of Apollo Creed, he daydreams of being in the ring with him and throwing a winning punch to the jaw.

Being victorous is a means of establishing status, and the struggle for status typically involves the use of aggression to create dominance, power, and security in a proactive manner. It's the fight part of the fight-or-flight impluse. An overt aggressive manner—even to the point of using violence or other forms of physical aggression—is probably more common of men. For women, acts of aggression may be physical but are probably more likely to be rendered verbally.

Harm Avoidance

This need reflects the passive retreat option in the fight-or-flight impulse. The central concern here is obviously securing safety—which becomes, in a mild form, a matter of seeking comfort.

In relation to Maslow's hierarchy of needs, there's a sure link between the second to lowest rung on the ladder—safety—and harm avoidance. Maslow's definition involves getting free from the threat of physical or emotional harm.

For Jensen, harm avoidance would equate to the emotional market of seeking peace of mind. Obvious business applications include banking and also home furnishings that reinforce a notion of security.

Underlying the harm avoidance need is the desire to find refuge. People don't want to find that all the motels have "no vacancy" signs as dusk approaches. We don't want to pick an unfamiliar vendor because, as some say, nobody ever got fired for hiring IBM.

The goal of harm avoidance can be viewed either in terms of pursuing safety or trying to avoid danger. Clearly, from an evolutionary perspective being able to recognize danger readily and elude risk enhances survival.

Most people are not risk-takers when they are comfortable with the status quo. As a species, humans have learned that a cautious approach most often increases chances for survival. Any change may be more risky than holding with what we already have. To make a mistake means suffering a loss.

For men, an active approach to harm avoidance may be more the norm. One advantage of playing video games and sports in general is that they sharpen the senses and arouse a little fear while letting one sharpen the ability to resolve danger on safe, favorable terms.

For women, harm avoidance can become a major need. This is true not only for themselves (in terms of fitting in) but also on behalf of others. They want to help their friends save face as well as protect their children. Men might gamble more with their investments, but women are often more focused on protective, safe, enduring relationships.

Example: For a big, well-known company like AT&T, playing up its advantage as a risk-free supplier of services makes good sense. One of their ads shows a pair of red dice tumbling toward the viewer on a craps table. Above copy that speaks about expertise worthy of trust, the headline reads: "Rolling the dice with your business communications?" AT&T thus offers a "safe bet" (business communications through them) instead of a risky gamble (another company).

Social Needs

The category I'm calling social needs consists of attachment and mating. What they have in common is the instinctive desire to belong to something greater than just ourselves, whether to family and the community at large (attachment) or in the enhanced intimacy of a romantic partnership (mating).

Attachment

The human need for attachment, and the corresponding distress at loss, represents another marketing avenue. Attachment is defined here as the desire for contact or union that involves one's family, friends, colleagues, or others. A particularly strong version of this need is represented by parent–infant attachment.

The middle rung on Maslow's hierarchy of needs is social needs. For him, it encompasses both attachment and mating and gets defined as a need for friends, a need to belong, and a need to give and receive love.

In Jensen's emotional markets schema, attachment fits nicely with the label of care-and-be-cared-for. His caring market ranges from pets, dolls, and toys to health care, medicine, and even the practice of religion. These are all opportunities to give or receive compassion and nurturing—in other words, the kind of emotionally based impulse that's not on the radar screen of rational, utilitarian-minded neoclassical economists.

Underlying this need is ultimately a desire for connection. The inverse is that when one experiences a sense of loss, it often involves nostalgia for a degree of belonging that was once enjoyed.

For men (who run high in testosterone), attachment is often not their strong suit. Separateness suits them better. But for women (who run high in hormones that aid the bonding and nurturing instincts), the opposite is generally true. Women are more likely to create relationships within the different arenas of

(continued)

their lives, enjoying associations within the work community, life-stage peer group, and so on. Women more instinctively structure social networks and build in avenues for attachment.

Another reason why women may also be more oriented to fulfilling the attachment need involves language skills. Studies show that girls learn to speak more quickly, master languages more readily, and generally have superior verbal skills compared with boys. Part of the reason for this probably lies in the brain structure. The corpus callosum is a group of fibers that connect the right and left hemispheres of the brain. The actual, narrow bridge-like structure that enacts the connection is larger in women than it is in men. Women are therefore probably better at sharing functions—including language—and they are more likely to gravitate to connective activities, which include gossip as a form of sharing information.

Example: A State Farm Insurance ad shows a tired young father, eyes closed, sitting in a rocking chair as he cradles a sleeping baby. The sensitive male presence has appeal for both genders. The ad exudes pure, caring attachment from photo to the tagline for the campaign, "We live where you live."

Mating (Sex)

Finally, the other major need is to achieve the enhanced physical and emotional intimacy of being in a relationship that involves or has the potential for romantic love, mating, and procreation. As with attachment, this need concerns a form of love—except that now the key unit is the couple instead of the family or a social network.

For Maslow, mating is part of social needs. For Jensen, mating would equate to what he calls the market for love (including friendship and togetherness). It's the market for companies whose offer helps people achieve emotional fulfillment and a sense of belonging.

Given his wide definition of this market, Jensen finds examples of companies responding to it with applications as diverse as telecommunications, bars, restaurants, clubs, coffee places, theme parks, camera and film companies, the funeral industry, beverages (especially liquor), lingerie and underwear, diamonds, the cosmetics industry, jewelry, home furnishings, music, movies, and clothing. Anything that helps unite people may qualify.

For most people, it seems to be part of human nature to interact with others rather than live as loners, and the innermost circle is to be in a romantic relationship. People long to love and be loved, but to realize this goal, we need to attract a mate and form a partnership.

In this romantic, sexual dynamic arises—most obviously—the gender gap. One has to wonder how far humans have progressed since the Stone Age when it comes to how courtship unfolds. For men, if there's a single word that would seem to describe what they are looking for, it is still *looks*—beauty, youth, and physical attractiveness. Men may pretend to the contrary, but desirability counts for a lot and men are more visually oriented than women. Meanwhile, for the women considering a man, ambition and energy, or at least competency and character, remain a good yardstick in determining how a man might measure up as a potential mate. What often gets measured? Beyond looks and (ideally) a sense of humor, women seek the ability and willingness to provide stable resources and protection.

There is now another angle for women who, over the past few decades, have maneuvered around the need for a man for survival.

Independent, financially secure, at liberty to choose wifehood and motherhood, many women are deferring, avoiding, or finding alternatives to marriage.

Good looks might sway women who, instead of scouting for a good provider, pursue romance and fantasize about intimate experiences. Note the growing number of fashion magazine ads that feature young, shirtless male models.

Male executives and creative directors face perhaps their largest blind spot in regard to mating. Research indicates that although men are energized by female nudity, women react by becoming tense and fatigued. Looks work for guys, period. Looks work for women when the ad suggests intimacy and relatedness.

Example: Reebok gets the attention of its target hip-hop audience with a bold black-and-white ad (see Figure 9.2). A woman in an animal print skirt is pressed into the corner of an elevator by a young man busy kissing her. The photo successfully highlights the shoes, and the only copy along with the Reebok label is the name of the shoe in large print. Though possibly too edgy for older consumers, the ad conveys energy to connect with the fantasy world of both genders of the so-called Y generation.

There are many potent ways to reach consumers, whether by appealing to innate desires, using sensory imagery that grips them and compels them to buy the product, or creating a brand story to draw them in and make them loyal. Ideally, you can use all of these tactics together into every touch point your company has with consumers. When done effectively, the results can be astonishing.

Stop button Classic

Figure 9.2 Reebok uses the innate desire for sex and mating to sell its Classics. The almost copy-free ad relies on the evocative photo to conjure associations of lust, intimacy, thrill, and fantasy—heightened by our awareness that this secret moment will end as soon as the elevator door opens. (Courtesy of Reebok, Bartle Bogle Hegarty. © Reebok International, Ltd.)

Notes

1. Edward Osborne Wilson, *Sociobiology: The New Synthesis* (Cambridge, MA: Harvard University Press, 2000); Steven Pinker, *The Blank Slate: The Modern Denial of Human Nature* (New York: Viking Press, 2002).

2. Rolf Jensen, *The Dream Society: How the Coming Shift from Information to Imagination Will Transform Your Business* (New York: McGraw-Hill, 1999), 51–113.

3. Paco Underhill, *Why We Buy: The Science of Shopping* (New York: Simon & Schuster, 1999), 98–128.

Looking Forward

How Science Will Continue to Benefit Marketing

In this final chapter, I discuss the present and future landscape for marketers. Many of these challenges may appear familiar. They include:

- A saturated marketplace that reduces a company's offer to a commodity;

- A fractured media arena that makes it harder to reach and connect with consumers;

- Consumers experiencing anxiety and information overload;

- The need to keep up with the pace of technology;

- The winner-takes-all syndrome;

- Avoiding expensive, hit-or-miss advertising campaigns;

(continued)

> - Heightened consumer expectations;
> - A lack of loyalty;
> - Crowded shelves;
> - Price wars.

The list goes on, but businesses can best withstand and profit from this welter of change and competing pressures by paying close attention to the human brain and the mind–body connection. The brain is probably the most complex organic structure on Earth and also the least understood. In the years ahead, scientists will undoubtedly announce new discoveries about cognition and communication.

What has been learned within even the past decade, however, is already enough to change the business model of how consumers make decisions and therefore how companies can build a more successful marketing strategy. The list of challenges just given illustrates the hard choices that much of the business world finds itself confronting right now, but companies can create a great advantage by accessing the human psyche.

For a company to benefit and continue to benefit from what science has learned, it needs to recognize the degree and manner in which consumers accept change, as well as the limits of hard-wired natures. Companies must take a wider view of how insights from evolutionary biology can be incorporated into business and the marketing realm. To be winners in tomorrow's marketplace, they should adhere to five major lessons from this book that I want to reiterate and pull together here in this final chapter. I will conclude by identifying three future changes and how they are likely to impact the business world.

> ## Lesson 1: Features-Based Marketing Is Futile
>
> The first major point to keep in mind is that rational, features-based marketing is becoming increasingly futile. The essential reasons why such an approach doesn't work well are a matter of biology and how humans are wired as a species. People simply don't respond as well to rational arguments as they do to offers that touch them emotionally.

Biological Reasons

Many unrecognized factors drive consumer decisions. By this I mean that we react on a mostly unconscious basis to stimuli that come from the environment, other people, our own actions, or memories of past experiences of a brand. This may seem like unnerving news, but the truth is that sensory clues put into motion a sense-feel-(think)-do decision-making process over which we have limited control. In fact, we're likely not even to know that a clue was taken in at all or whether it's the one generating the primary response.

The implications of this process for marketing is that the carefully prepared arguments that an advertisement may set forth may be already colored by the sensory elements of the ad or they may not be noticed at all, enough, or in time to motivate consideration and influence purchase behavior.

A second biological factor that negatively impacts the viability of features-based marketing is that the crucial leopard brain, which drives sensory-emotive reactions, is oriented to threats and thrills. The autonomic nervous system involves several subsystems, including sympathetic reactions that excite and mobilize us (the fight-or-flight response), and parasympathetic reactions that tend to relax us by counteracting the effects of the sympathetic nervous system. The upshot of this wiring is that, as a species, humans are biologically built for short periods of strenuous activity, then long periods of rest and relaxation.

Human bodies were designed for a lifestyle more like that of a housecat. We respond quickly and intuitively to whatever sparks fear or happiness. We're not wired to act like a computer that checks off the variables as it considers whether an offer makes rational sense.

Sociological Reasons

In an increasingly media-driven world wherein people thrive on entertainment, a marketing approach that relies on making a reasoned argument runs the risk of sounding like a lecture.

For example, a Web site that features an engrossing video will overwhelm any kind of informational copy around it. Likewise, it is becoming ever more the norm to switch channels at will. A TV remote control and the apparent increase in attention deficit disorders serve as apt metaphors for the world today. Whatever strikes consumers as long, boring, or confusing gets zapped off the screen, and few people are willing to listen to explanations for reasons that involve greater degrees of both cynicism and stress.

> ## Lesson 2: Consumer Responses Are Driven by Visceral Clues
>
> Rational-based marketing isn't as effective as marketing oriented to how humans are programmed to think and make decisions. So to maximize marketing success, orient your approach to intuitive, gut-level consumer responses. Consumers react to products on a visceral level, using the intimacy of the product experience to judge on a more unconscious basis if that experience feels right. Whether a product or promotion is the focal point, companies need to capitalize on what science has now unearthed about the brain and how the mind–body connection works.

Sensory Considerations

Verbal language is more rational, abstract, and linear. People have to decode a vocabulary of symbols. Perceptual logic is more intuitive, concrete, and immediate.

> *On a sensory basis, humans establish the cause-and-effect meaning of a clue through the patterns, associations, relationships and dimensionality on display for the senses to grasp. As a result, people process sensory perceptions differently than they do verbal language. By using the senses to evaluate a company's offer or projected profile, we draw on an "elaborate and secret code that is written nowhere, known by none, and understood by all."*[1]

To emphasize price and features misses 80 percent of the communication opportunity with consumers. How should a company manage the sensory connection? By choosing sensory metaphors that differentiate it from the color schemes and other sensory patterns of rivals, in particular the category leader if that slot belongs to somebody else.

Emotional Considerations

Companies focus on encouraging happiness when they should be at least as concerned about off-setting fear.

A case in point: When you walk into a store, and especially if you hesitate at all in moving around, you're likely to be asked by a clerk if he or she can help you.

The problem with this well-meaning question is that it inspires fear. It has the effect of putting the consumer in the inferior position of seemingly needing assistance or of being in uncharted territory and therefore vulnerable. To need help is, for one thing, a state that triggers the fear of getting taken advantage of or looking stupid.

The default response is to reject the offer of help. A fear of failure causes us to tell ourselves, in effect, *I don't do this. I don't deal with anything new.* Aloud, we tell the clerk, "No thanks," and move on. Generating reassurance—not happiness—is job one in business.

Lesson 3: Revisit Marketing Research

The third major point to keep in mind to position your company for future growth is to secure a new

(continued)

---

type of marketing research that will better reflect and gauge how consumers actually make their decisions. Getting access to intuitive responses is the key because then you will be in familiar territory.

Humans are hard-wired to respond to objects, people, settings, and situations in certain, largely prescribed ways. The role of marketing research should be to help a company identify and leverage those natural, biologically driven orientations.

Speak Visually

Whatever the mode of research employed, it must honor the reality that consumers think in images, not words. Asking in an online survey or focus group session, "What is this ad saying to you?" or "What's the message?" or "What's the value or benefit of this product?" enables at best a partial answer to how the consumer is responding. Most understanding and therefore response to a stimulus come through the senses, especially the eyes, and research must follow suit.

A new marketing medium like the Web offers an opportunity to start fresh. Efforts to trace not only the navigational path and duration of viewing given pages but also the specific point of visual focus provide a model for where marketing research must go on a perceptual basis.

Once the points of interest have been identified, the real work must begin. Besides determining whether the other senses are being appropriately utilized, marketing research must help establish whether the visuals are generating not only initial interest and sustained appeal but also whether they create an overall signature style.

Because people are geared toward what's either novel and fresh or familiar, companies can't afford to downplay the importance of providing a familiar, signature look and feel in their communications. (This signature look is, of course, the essence of branding.)

Too often, advertising retains only the brand name and the logo from one campaign to another. As a result, companies perhaps unknowingly dismiss the value of providing consumers with familiar elements like a color scheme, layout format, music, symbols, and other devices that feed into the associative network people form over time using their senses. An important way in which marketing research can provide value is by ensuring the stable use of those elements that are best able to foster a deep connection with consumers.

There are several truths about emotions that marketing research must come to terms with, including the following:

- Things perceived to be obscure create discomfort. Therefore, marketing needs to be easy, simple, and highly accessible. People want to see, understand, and feel good about the offer.

- The biggest lies are the ones people tell themselves; hence, fat-free ice cream sells because of hope. What people feel resonates more than what they think.

(continued)

> We crave things that appear familiar. Well-known stimuli serve as shorthand, triggering what's already inside us and, therefore, accepted.

Understand Emotions

Women seek connections, whereas men seek release. This dichotomy is obviously a stereotype, but it's one that is also frequently accurate. Therefore, in forming a signature style, a company must take into account the mentality of its target audience and the emotional dynamic it seeks to create to link the company, its offer, and consumers. Reporting on customer satisfaction is inevitably only a start. To be of real help to a company, marketing research must get better not only at speaking visually but also at understanding emotions.

Lesson 4: The Brand Story Is a Great Asset

The fourth major point to keep in mind to adopt a future-oriented brand strategy is that the world is becoming increasingly impersonal. Because people have lost much of the sense of community, the sense of being truly, deeply connected with others, they compensate in part by seeking to connect with brands. In fact, many communities grow up around some of the most compelling brands, as seen in the Harley-

(continued)

Davidson culture and the devotion of fans to their favorite rock-and-roll bands.

In response to this desire for a familiar relationship, a brand story offers a powerful way for companies to captivate consumers and keep them coming back for more. Companies that have successfully created an effective brand story are at a distinct advantage because they've achieved familiarity and earned consumers' trust. They must carefully develop their brands and the brand story, but half of the battle is already won.

The Gender Gap

Men say they weigh facts over feelings, but women typically admit that they prefer feeling-based stories. Women still do the majority of the shopping, and they are the majority of the readers of romance novels and fiction of all kinds, as well as the primary viewers of soap operas.

Women often welcome the intimacy of a story, and companies would be wise to provide it. Meanwhile, men aren't as immune to stories as they want to believe they are; they often feel more comfortable with the nonfiction variety, involving sport stars, spies, military figures, and other heroes.

Whether appealing to men or to women, companies need to realize and take advantage of the human tendency to get caught up in a great story. Stories provide a vicarious escape, and they also enable us to judge things, form opinions, and better understand the world.

Implicit Stories

Stories can crop up in places where one might not expect to find them. For instance, a restaurant near a shoreline is likely to enjoy an advantage because of the aesthetics of watching the waves. Furthermore, although the restaurant owners might not realize it, their real estate appeals to deeply ingrained biological drives for the following reason: Eating a meal relates to foraging, a key evolutionary need, and in the act of hunting our ancestors learned that a body of water not only took care of their own thirst but also typically attracted wild animals they could capture and eat. So, bodies of water and food naturally go together.

In a similar fashion, emotions also have their own built-in story lines. The heated mind/body reaction that accompanies anger isn't, in the end, about summoning the energy to destroy a barrier to progress so much as it is about restoring an injured sense of self-worth.

The behavior and psychological themes associated with any emotion are fairly predictable, and companies would do well to work with the emotive scripts pertinent to their offers. Moreover, these emotions feed into the overall brand story, making it even more efficacious.

Lesson 5: Constantly Enrich the Connection with Consumers

The fifth and final major point to keep in mind to position your company for future growth is that you can tap into the hard-wired evolutionary psychology of consumers in more than one way. Yes, directly addressing their needs serves as one approach. But it is also possible to drive the relevancy of the offer more indirectly, by drawing on the sensory metaphors outlined earlier. These metaphors aid marketing campaigns by providing both the supportive context and the immediacy that consumers require to be sold.

Invoke the Pattern

A branded offer provides its own sensory clues through its promotion and the experience that the product's design and usage supplies for consumers. However, those clues never stand alone—they inevitably intersect with and are influenced by previous, specific experiences of either the branded offer or other offers in the category, as well as by the general, fundamental perceptual classifications that have evolved in us over time as a species.

Therefore, the branded offer must be careful to create an associative pattern that invokes rather than goes against the grain of the larger, established patterns that lie embedded within the collective psyche.

For instance, if "small" works for technology products because it signals nimble speed and efficiency, there is no marketing sense in trying to make "tall and bulky" into a desirable physical attribute on behalf of your company's offer.

Whether applied to advertising or product design, establishing an appropriate pattern is essential because consumers recognize the familiar quickly and easily. People are biased in favor of cognitive consistency because it involves less work, and we tend to reject anything that doesn't fit in readily with what we already know or have come to expect.

In other words, to engage in marketing without invoking a mental model runs the risk that there's no memory address to which you can send the sensory-emotive envelope in which you have enclosed your offer.

Go Deep, Not Wide

Emotions are immediate and set the stage for the decision-making process. We can't necessarily articulate trust, for example, but we can tell whether or not we feel it. Such emotional resonance happens spontaneously, and it is triggered by sensory clues or metaphors that are either being experienced for the first time or being retrieved from memory.

> *Emotional responses happen spontaneously; we tend to move on to the next set of stimuli after about two seconds. However, scientists have found that humans take three times as long to process less familiar words; this statistic accounts for why there's danger involved in being too obscure.*

Bombarding consumers with a multitude of sensory signals doesn't work well, either. The more they have to take in, the greater the likelihood that their mental processing will be too shallow to inspire an affinity for the offer and the ability to recall it from memory. The greatest opportunity for seizing and holding the attention of consumers lies in presenting an offer that's just slightly askance of what is expected.

Looking Ahead: Three Future Developments

Where is brand marketing headed? Early in this new millennium, words like *saturation, speed,* and *plasticity* (as in flexibility) come readily to mind. It's safe to predict that getting a sensory-emotive foothold with consumers will only become more difficult over time. The best way to counter that predicament will be to respect the low road of consumers' emotionally based decision making rather than trying to travel on the high, rationally based road alone.

Other relatively safe but no less important predications about the future include the following.

Anticipate Increased Fragmentation and Customization

Many remarkable new tools are allowing marketers to tailor messages to consumers. In fact, many companies have now begun to offer "smart" billboards that can electronically read the radio station playing in a car and from that make a fairly educated guess about the type of listener in the car. In response, the billboard will show whatever message best fits the largest spectrum of consumers that happen to be passing by at that particular moment. The fact that there are scores of radio stations isn't much of a technological hindrance.

Marketing will have to tackle new challenges as technology enables greater customization that will lead to an ever more fragmented marketplace.

Consumers are increasingly blocking out advertising messages, both mentally and through the use of popular products like TiVo, a digital video recorder. In the future, we're all going to be living in our own wired worlds, and companies are going to have to follow suit by making their marketing efforts more customized. Appealing to consumers' emotional bandwidth and biological drives is one way companies can break into these insular environments.

Expect More and Better Data about Consumers

Data are no substitute for knowledge, but it's a start. In the future, the ability to customize marketing is certain to benefit from more and better data about consumers. Some data are likely to be provided through computerized searches and the cross-indexing of variables, but additional brain discoveries are just as likely to provide new markers and ways to read the all-important unconscious mind.

For example, FedEx has already given its workers wearable computers that help them keep better track of shipments and other logistical matters. With wireless technology and the miniaturization of components, there's a high probability that within the next decade or so, marketing research will routinely begin to test consumer reactions, using high-tech, mobile, real-time methods.

Build Global Products and Local Stories

The global community found on the World Wide Web stands as a preview for the globalization that's becoming increasingly important to all businesses. In the coming years, energy giants like ExxonMobil will earn well over half their income overseas, and companies as diverse as Coca-Cola, Johnson & Johnson, Kodak, and Goodyear Tire and Rubber have committed to generating more revenue abroad.

With lower barriers to products traveling across borders, however, comes the problem of companies not easily able to understand marketplaces far removed from corporate headquarters. The need for local, customized marketing and brand stories that speak to regional and national differences while also complementing the larger global brand story will be imperative, especially given sensitivities about the combined weight of America's economic, military, and cultural power.

Concluding Thoughts

With or without technology and whether at home or abroad, ideally the future will involve the marketing and marketing research departments working more closely early in the creative process with internal product development teams and external advertising agencies. The goal is to gain front-end insights that help create the sensory-emotive connection that's most persuasive.

My prediction for marketing is that radical simplicity will become increasingly expected and valued. Second, I see campaigns of the future as deep, real, and caring. Finally, there are lots of stories already out there, the biggest and the most basic of which remains the search for love.

One last note: Don't think of the interaction as merely a transaction, because even consumers who won't admit it yearn for greater appreciation. A company will never go wrong by making its customers feel valued.

The challenge for all companies is learning how to quickly establish a long-term relationship. Whether you are wooing a prospective spouse or a potential customer, it's all the same dance.

Continually manage the sensory connection and use visible, tangible clues to establish a lasting bond.

Note

1. Laurence Wiley, *Beaux Gestes* (Cambridge, MA: Undergraduate Press, E. P. Dutton, 1977).

ACKNOWLEDGMENTS

This book is the result of over half a decade of research, thinking, and bringing into business practice the concepts, tools, and methodologies that harness the power of the sensory-emotive connection.

Once the process began in earnest, I had the good luck to have lots of talented people come into my life to aid in honing an approach. In the early development phase, I learned about possible psychophysiological tools through a high school soccer buddy, Tom Finholt, now at the University of Michigan. In understanding biofeedback, I had the aid of Dick Gevirtz at Alliant International University. I met with Paul Ekman at the University of California, San Francisco, on a couple of occasions, and we shared additional e-mails and phone conversations. Andrew Ortony at Northwestern University has been an ongoing source of insights, working models, and welcome humor.

In establishing Sensory Logic, I have enjoyed the talents and personalities of Michael Vickroy, Denise Hawkinson, Carolyn Springer, Margo Parker, Rachelle Rene, Todd Kringlie, Karma Forester, Jill Saxty, Laurie Marrelli, Jason Holden, Eric Carr, and, last but not least, Simone Paul, among others over the years.

In creating this book, I had the aid of Diane Norman, Kathryn Mathews, Mary Beckman, and Kate Hanning Olson for read-throughs. Thanks also to Paul Samuel Schuster, whose thorough review of this book's early drafts helped me sift out the big themes, making the material more accessible to a wide range of readers. Maura Williams, on staff, was my layout artist of extraordinary patience and added insights and perspectives, especially regarding gender differences. Jeff Herman has been my faithful agent, and Airié Stuart and Jessica Noyes saw an idea for a manuscript they couldn't resist.

Thanks to my dad for his integrity, high standards, and business acumen. Thanks to my mom for taking me to art museums and turning me on to aesthetics from a young age. Two former work colleagues and long-term friends have been instrumental as well. The first is Jack Murphy, who has taken part in the business and who read drafts as my ever-skeptical Irishman.

That leaves Joe Rich. How lucky I am. His boundless energy, good cheer, great heart, sage advice, and emotional investment in my endeavor have been so far beyond commendable as to be downright embarrassingly generous.

Index